POSITIVE DISCIPLINE

A doctorate in psychology is secondary to the education and experience Jane Nelsen achieved from her successes and failures as a mother of seven children. Dr. Nelsen is a marriage, family, and child therapist in Fair Oaks, California. For ten years she was a college instructor in child development and director of Project ACCEPT (Adlerian Counseling Concepts for Encouraging Parents and Teachers) where she had the opportunity to teach and learn from thousands of parents and teachers. She now shares this wealth of knowledge and experience in lectures and workshops throughout the world.

POSITIVE DISCIPLINE

This extraordinary book has already reached a vast audience and has gained praise in America and abroad. Please turn the page for some of the glowing testimonials from both parents and educators. . . .

"When parents and teachers use the ideas, processes, and techniques described herein, the results are remarkable. Students don't want to run away from school—they want to run to school."

J. W. Rollings, Ed. D.
Parent/Educator

"Your book has changed my life in the classroom—and my whole attitude toward teaching. It has helped by teaching my students to take on social and academic responsibility. During class meetings students learn language skills through orderly public speaking, social studies skills through self-government, and classroom management skills which improve the total academic atmosphere of the classroom."

Gene Ford
Eighth Grade Teacher
Sacramento, California

"Jane has been a keynote speaker at P.E.N. (Parent Education Network) Conferences, has done training of trainers, and we use *Positive Discipline* for parent education classes. Participant evaluations have shown excellent ratings in all three areas."

Muriel Kelleher
Executive Director, P.E.N.
Chico, California

"I have been using [this] book in workshops with teachers—they love it! . . . It is exciting to see the improvements that have been made over the years with these marvelous ideas. You have made a valuable contribution."

Bob Bradbury, M. Div.
Pastor
Admiral Congregational U.C.C.,
Seattle, Washington

"No one is perfect, but Jane Nelsen describes in an understandable way how we can have an almost perfect relationship with our children."

Angelike Jager
Parent
Bod Soden, Germany

"Walnut Grove Elementary School in Pleasanton, California, adopted *Positive Discipline* in the fall of 1981. Teachers enthusiastically used class meetings and experienced dramatic results. As principal, I facilitated several parent study groups. The net result was a school full of happy teachers, students, and parents working together in an atmosphere of cooperation to solve problems and improve social and academic skills. I cannot speak highly enough of this program and its benefits."

Robert W. Wakeling
Superintendent
Sunol Glenn School District, California

POSITIVE DISCIPLINE

Jane Nelsen, Ed. D.

BALLANTINE BOOKS · NEW YORK

Originally published by Sunrise Press, Fair Oaks, California in 1981.
Grateful acknowledgment is made for permission to reprint the following:
"Matthew" by John Denver. © copyright 1974 by Cherry Lane Music Publishing Company, Inc. All rights reserved. Used by permission.
Library of Congress Catalog Card Number: 87-91180
ISBN: 0-345-34856-7
Cover design by Richard Aquan
Photo: Edward Tsutsumi
Text design by Holly Johnson

Manufactured in the United States of America

First Ballantine Books Edition: August 1987
10 9 8 7 6 5

To Barry

Who taught me what it means to experience the
encouragement of total love and acceptance

CONTENTS

Foreword by H. Stephen Glenn, Ph.D.   xiii
Positive Discipline Guidelines   xvii
Preface and Acknowledgments   xxi
Introduction   3
  1. The Positive Approach   8
  2. Some Basic Concepts   21
  3. The Significance of Birth Order   31
  4. Four Mistaken Goals of Behavior   46
  5. Natural and Logical Consequences   67
  6. Using Encouragement Effectively   87
  7. Class Meetings   114
  8. Family Meetings   144
  9. Putting It All Together   160
10. Love and Joy in Families and Schools   189
Appendixes   211
  Peer Counseling   213
  Starting a Study Group   218

Sample Flyer   219
Study Group Schedule   220
Group Participation   222
Problem-Solving Form   225
Using the Problem-Solving Form   226
Problem-Solving Possibilities   229
Class-Meeting Observation Form   231
A Little Imperfection Song   232
Suggested Readings   233
Index   235

FOREWORD

For thousands of years parents and teachers learned the art of raising children through grandmothers, grandfathers, aunts, uncles, and neighbors who lived together under relatively stable circumstances for generations.

When changes became necessary, the value of sharing wisdom and experiences was instinctively understood by the pilgrims and pioneers, who traveled together and settled communities with common values and community goals.

Suddenly, at the end of World War II there was a mass migration from small towns and farm communities into urban and suburban environments. An entire culture was dislocated due to the combined effects of the Industrial Revolution, the GI Bill, reaction to the Depression, and technology. The wisdom and support of extended family and long-time friends was lost.

Soon after this dramatic shift to urban communities,

nearly eleven million couples began giving birth to an average of 4.2 children each and became urban pioneers crossing a frontier of life-style and technology without networks and support systems to offer an accumulation of wisdom to guide them.

Not knowing they were pioneers, these couples forgot the basic strategy that had enabled other pioneers to successfully colonize a new continent. They forgot that pioneers got together with strangers around the campfire to compare notes on the journey so that everyone didn't have to perish learning the same lessons. Instead of following the wisdom of generations who relied on learning from each other, they became isolated.

Those who did not replace family and community support systems with networks of fellow travelers often covered feelings of inadequacy and lack of knowledge about what to do with a false sense of pride in "handling their own problems." They adopted the belief that people shouldn't discuss family business with strangers. It became important to them to hide their problems and handle them, often very ineffectively, behind closed doors. They traded in wisdom and principles acquired over centuries for books and theories untried and untested.

At the same time a national fantasy grew up that the only thing between Americans and a generation of perfect, super children was perfect, super parents. What a shock when many children did not turn out perfectly. The guilt, stress, and denial tore people apart.

Parenting, which was once the cumulative work of generations, became a grim, part-time struggle for two or more relatives who did not have much experience in what they were trying to do.

Statistics show that the approximately 4.3 million children born in 1946 overpowered urban schools in 1951. They took the achievement tests in 1963 and reversed a three-hundred-year upward trend. In all areas of achievement, children had been improving up until this time. The children who were born after World War II started a downward trend in achievement and an upward trend in crime, teenage pregnancy, clinical depression, and suicide.

Clearly, our understanding of and resources for raising and educating children was compromised by urbanization and technology.

In her book, *Positive Discipline,* Jane Nelsen has gathered up the wisdom of many pioneers ahead of her and has created a warm campfire for parents and teachers who desire timeless principles that work, instead of theories that do not.

In this book, Jane gives a very practical set of guidelines for parents and teachers who wish to help their children develop self-discipline, responsibility, and positive capabilities and attitudes.

I think enough of Jane's book that it has been adopted as a text in our internationally recognized training program, Developing Capable People, which is used throughout North and Central America and Africa. The principles work and provide a wonderful basis for the enrichment of the family experience.

H. Stephen Glenn, Ph.D.
President, Capabilities Incorporated
Lexington, South Carolina
November 1985

POSITIVE DISCIPLINE GUIDELINES

1. Misbehaving children are *discouraged* children, who have mistaken ideas on how to achieve their primary goal—*to belong*. Their mistaken ideas lead them to misbehavior.

2. Use *encouragement* to help children feel a sense of belonging so that the motivation for misbehaving will be eliminated.

3. A great way to help children feel encouraged is to spend special time being with them, doing something you can enjoy together. With younger children this could be fifteen minutes a day. With older children it could be an hour once a week.

4. When tucking children into bed ask them to *share with you* their "saddest time" during the day and their "happiest time" during the day. Then *share with them*. You will be surprised what you learn.

5. Have *family meetings* to solve problems with cooper-

ation and mutual respect. This is the key to creating a loving family atmosphere while helping children develop self-discipline, responsibility, cooperation, and problem-solving skills.

6. Give children *meaningful chores.* Many children would rather cook than wash dishes. Children feel a sense of belonging when they know they can make a real contribution.

7. *Decide together* what chores need to be done. Put them all in a jar and let each child draw out a few each week. Then no one is stuck with the same chores all the time.

8. *Take time for training.* Make sure children understand what "clean the kitchen" means to you. To them it may mean simply putting the dishes in the sink.

9. Get rid of the crazy idea that in order to make children do better, first you have to make them feel worse. *Do you feel like doing better when you feel humiliated?*

10. *Punishment may work if all you are interested in is stopping misbehavior for the moment. Sometimes we must beware of what works* when the long-range results are negative—resentment, rebellion, revenge, or retreat.

11. *Teach and model mutual respect.* One way is to be kind and firm at the same time—kind to show respect for the child, and firm to show respect for yourself and the needs of the situation. This is difficult during conflict, so use the next step first.

12. Proper timing will improve your effectiveness tenfold. It does not work to deal with a problem at the time of conflict—emotions get in the way. Teach children about *cooling-off periods.* You or the children can go to a separate room and do something to make yourself feel better—and then work on the problem with mutual respect.

13. Use logical consequences when appropriate. Follow the Three Rs of Logical Consequences to make sure consequences are *related, respectful,* and *reasonable.*

14. During family meetings *children can help decide* on logical consequences for not keeping their agreements. (Remember not to use the word *punishment,* which does not work for long-range "good" results.)

15. Avoid morning hassles by *establishing routines* the night before, such as having children choose their clothes and lay them out, along with books, shoes, etc. Help children decide how much time they need to get ready and allow them responsibility to get up, with their own alarm clock. Allow them to experience the consequences if they are late.

16. Learn the Four Steps for Winning Cooperation: (a) Guess how your child is feeling. Get into your child's world. Check with your child to see if your guess is correct. (b) Show understanding. You don't have to agree or condone to understand. If possible, share an example of a time when you felt the same. (c) Share your feelings about the situation in a nonaccusing manner, using "I" messages. Children are willing to hear you *after* they feel heard. (d) Work together on ideas to avoid the problem in the future—or to correct the present problem through a logical consequence. If the first three steps have been done in a respectful manner, your child will be ready for cooperation in the fourth step.

17. Model *recovery* after you make mistakes. Share with your child what you didn't like about your behavior and ask for help in finding a better solution.

18. Teach children that *mistakes are wonderful opportunities to learn!*

PREFACE AND ACKNOWLEDGMENTS

Positive Discipline is based on the philosophy and teachings of Alfred Adler and Rudolph Dreikurs. I was not privileged to study under either of these great men, but I would like to acknowledge the people who introduced me to the Adlerian approach. It has changed my life and greatly improved my relationships with children at home and in the classroom.

I am the mother of seven children. Many years ago, when I had only five children, including two teenagers, I was frustrated by the same childrearing problems experienced by so many parents today. I did not know how to get my children to stop fighting with each other, to pick up their toys, or to complete the chores they had promised to do. I had problems getting them to bed at night—and then getting them up in the morning. They didn't want to get into the tub—and then didn't want to get out. Mornings were miserable, for it seemed impossible to get them off to school without constant reminders and irritating hassles. After school was a continuation of battles over homework and chores. My "bag of tricks" included threatening, yelling, and spanking. These methods felt terrible to me and my children—and they didn't work. I was threatening, yelling, and spanking for the same misbehaviors over and over again. This became very clear to me one day as I heard myself repeating, "I've told you a hundred times to pick up your toys." It suddenly dawned on me who the real "dummy" was— and it wasn't my children. How ridiculous that it took me one hundred times to realize my approach wasn't working! And how frustrating because I didn't know what else to do.

Compounding my dilemma was my status as a senior in college, majoring in Child Development. I was reading many wonderful books that expounded the many fantastic things I should be accomplishing with my children; but none of them explained how to achieve these lofty goals.

Imagine my relief when on the first day of a new class I heard that we were not going to learn many new theories, but would thoroughly investigate the Adlerian approach, including skills for practical application to help children stop misbehaving.

To my delight, it worked. I was able to reduce fighting among my children by at least 80 percent. I learned to eliminate morning and bedtime hassles and to achieve much greater cooperation in the completion of chores. The most important change was that I found I enjoyed being a mother most of the time.

I was so enthusiastic that I wanted to share these ideas with others. My first opportunity was with a group of parents of educationally, physically, and mentally handicapped children.

At first the parents of these children were reluctant to try these methods. They were afraid their children would not be able to learn self-discipline, responsibility, and cooperation. Many parents of handicapped children do not understand how clever all children can be at manipulation. The parents in this group soon learned how disrespectful they were being to their children by pampering them rather than helping them develop their full potential.

I was subsequently employed as a counselor in the Elk Grove Unified School District in Elk Grove, California, where many parents, teachers, psychologists, and administrators were supportive of Adlerian concepts to increase effectiveness with children at home and in the classroom. I am especially grateful to Dr. John Platt, psychologist, whom I adopted as my mentor. He taught me a great deal.

Dr. Don Larson, assistant superintendent, and Dr. Platt were responsible for obtaining a Title IV-C grant and received Federal funding to develop an Adlerian Counseling Program. I was fortunate to be chosen as the director of this program. During the three years of developmental funding, the program was so effective in teaching parents and teachers to help children change their misbehavior that the program achieved recognition as an exemplary project and received a three-year grant for dissemination to school districts in California. We adopted the name Project A.C.C.E.P.T. (Adlerian Counseling Concepts for Encouraging Parents and Teachers). Through this experience I had the opportunity to share Adlerian concepts with thousands of parents and teachers. I learned a great deal from them as they shared stories of how they used the skills they had learned in the Project Accept training workshops. I gratefully acknowledge those who gave me permission to share their examples with others. Special thanks go to Frank Meder for his contributions in the area of class meetings. He was able to grasp and implement a very important principle—that freedom is impossible in a social environment without equal emphasis on order.

Acknowledgement and sincere appreciation go to those who worked as paraprofessionals for Project Accept. Susan Anderson, Judi Dixon, George Montgomery, Ann Platt, Barbara Smellie, Marjorie Spiak, and Vicky Zirkle worked tirelessly as leaders of parent study groups while organizing and developing materials used in the project. They all shared many examples of the effectiveness of the principles with their own families and the families with whom they worked.

My children have been sources of inspiration, opportunity, and love. I refer to them as my before, during, and after children. Terry and Jim were already teenagers when I learned about these concepts. Kenny, Bradley, and Lisa were seven, five, and three respectively. Mark and Mary were born after I had been teaching parent study groups for a while. They are the subjects of many examples. The greatest benefit of all has come from the understanding of principles that increased mutual respect, cooperation, enjoyment, and love.

POSITIVE
DISCIPLINE

INTRODUCTION

Some books on discipline are written for parents. Others are written for teachers. This book is written for both because:

· The concepts are the same for parents and teachers. The only difference is the setting in which they are applied.

· Many teachers are also parents who would like to use these concepts at home and at school.

· Understanding and cooperation between home and school is increased when parents and teachers both are united in their methods of helping children and each other in positive ways.

This book will explain a theory that will help increase your understanding of children, as well as techniques for practical application that will help children learn self-discipline, responsibility, problem-solving skills, and co-operation.

Throughout this book examples are given of how Positive Discipline principles have been used effectively in homes and schools. Once you understand the principles, your common sense and intuition will enable you to apply them in your own life.

When we seem to lose sight of our own common sense in dealing with our children, it can be helpful to read a book or talk with others who can offer perspective. At times, it seems easier to have perspective on someone else's situation than our own. For this reason organizing a parent or teacher study group can be helpful. A group can offer invaluable moral support and the encouragement needed for changing old habits and learning new skills.

But bear in mind that Positive Discipline and group participation are not meant to replace your own common sense. The principles and suggestions you receive from others will be most effective when they serve as reminders and guides to what you already know intuitively. When Positive Discipline principles are enacted from feeling of uncertainty or doubt, they will not be effective.

Bear in mind, too, that in learning to apply the Positive Discipline principles, you will make some mistakes. But mistakes are not necessarily bad. They can be great learning opportunities. The important thing is to learn from our mistakes so that we become even better because of them.

Each chapter in Positive Discipline ends with discussion questions that serve to deepen understanding. The appendixes offer some hints for successful group facilitation. A group may consist of as few as two people or as many as ten. If the group gets larger than that there is less opportunity for individual involvement.

The universal reaction of parents and teachers who attend study groups is, "What a relief to know I'm not the only one who is experiencing frustration!" It is comforting to know that others are in the same boat.

Study-group members will also be in the same boat when group facilitators make it clear that they are not experts. Groups are much more effective if no one assumes the role of an expert. A group leader or co-leaders take responsibility for asking the questions and keeping the group on task—not for providing the answers. If no one in the group knows the answer to a question, allow time to find it in the book.

The responsibility of group members is to read the chapters, be prepared to discuss the questions, and cooperate with the leaders by staying "on task." If a group member has not found time to read the assigned chapter, he or she can nevertheless benefit from listening to the discussion.

It is not necessary to accept all the principles at once. Use only what makes sense to you at the time. And if you hear something that does not seem right to you, don't throw out the baby with the bath water. Some concepts that seem difficult to accept or understand now might make more sense later. One group member said that she tried some of the principles on her son, just to prove that they were wrong, and was surprised to see the positive change in their relationship. She later became a parent study group leader because she wanted to share these concepts that had helped her so much.

As you begin to use Positive Discipline principles, remember that children are used to getting certain re-

sponses from adults as a result of their behavior. They
know how we are going to react and are disappointed if
we don't live up to their expectations, even when the
reaction is negative. It is similar to what most of us do
when we put our money in a soda machine that doesn't
work. When we don't get our expected soda, we kick and
pound on the machine to try to make it do what it is
supposed to do. When we begin to change our responses,
children will probably exaggerate their misbehavior (get
worse) in their effort to get us to respond as we are
"supposed to." However, if we are kind and firm in our
new responses, children will learn that their misbehavior
does not achieve the responses they are expecting and
will be motivated to change their behavior.

It is helpful to have patience with ourselves and with
our children as we try to change old habits. As our understanding of the underlying principles deepens, practical
application becomes easier. Patience, humor, and forgiveness enhance our learning process.

Positive Discipline principles can be compared to a
puzzle with many concepts (pieces). It is difficult to see
the whole picture until you have all or most of the pieces.
Sometimes one concept does not make sense until you
combine it with another concept or attitude. For example
logical consequences is not effective without being
kind and firm at the same time.

A FEW PIECES OF THE PUZZLE

Natural and Logical Consequences
Understanding the Four Goals of Misbehavior
Kindness and Firmness at the same time

Mutual Respect
Family and Class Meetings
Encouragement

It is suggested that study groups wait until after they have covered the material in the first six chapters before working on specific problem situations. You will then have enough knowledge to help each other with the practical application of ideas.

There is a problem-solving form in the appendixes to use as a guide for discussing specific situations. Group facilitators might like to copy several of these forms to distribute to each member during the first session. When someone brings up a specific problem during the first few sessions, group leaders can suggest that it be written down for discussion later. Knowing that they will be able to discuss specific situations later will encourage group members to stay on task and cover all the material.

One more word of caution: Try only one new technique at a time. You will be learning many new concepts and skills that will take practice for successful application. It can be confusing and discouraging to expect too much of yourself. Apply one technique at a time and move ahead slowly, remembering to see mistakes as opportunities to learn.

Many parents and teachers have found that even though their children don't become perfect, they enjoy them much more after applying these concepts and attitudes. This is my wish for you.

Chapter One

THE POSITIVE APPROACH

If you are a teacher, have you been teaching long enough to remember when children sat in neat rows and obediently did what they were told?

If you are a parent, do you remember when children wouldn't dare talk back to their parents?

Many parents and teachers today are feeling frustrated because children don't behave the way they used to in "the good old days."

What happened? Why don't today's children develop the same kind of responsibility and motivation that seemed more prevalent in youth many years ago?

Theorists offer many possible explanations, such as broken homes, too much television, and working mothers. Since these factors are so common in our society today, the situation would seem rather hopeless if they actually served to explain our current problems with children. Fortunately, there are other major changes that have taken place in society over the past few years that are more directly related. And the outlook is very hopeful because, with awareness and desire, we can compensate for these changes and in doing so can also eliminate some of the problems that are caused by broken homes, too much television, and working mothers.

The first major change is that adults no longer give children an example or model of submission and obedience. Adults forget that they no longer act the way they used to in the good old days.

Remember when Mom obediently did whatever Dad said, or at least gave the impression she did, because it was the culturally acceptable thing to do? In the good old days few people questioned the idea that Dad's decisions were final. Because of the human-rights movement, this is no longer true. When Mom quit modeling submissiveness, children stopped being submissive. Rudolph Dreikurs pointed out, "When Dad lost control of Mom, they both lost control of the children."

In the good old days there were many models of submission. Even Dad obeyed the boss so he wouldn't lose his job. Today all minority groups are actively claiming their rights to full equality and dignity. It is difficult to find anyone who is willing to accept an inferior, submissive role in life. Children are simply following the examples all around them.

The desire for dignity and respect is a very positive change in our society. We simply need to be aware of the significance of this change and realize that today cooperation based on mutual respect and shared responsibility is more effective than authoritarian control.

Another major change is that in today's society children have fewer opportunities to learn responsibility and motivation. We no longer "need" children as important contributors to economic survival. Instead children are given too much without any effort or investment on their part. We often rob children of opportunities to feel belonging and significance in meaningful ways through responsible contributions and then complain and and criticize them for not developing responsibility. We need to provide opportunities for children to experience responsibility in direct relationship to the privileges they enjoy. Otherwise, they become dependent recipients who feel the only way to achieve belonging and significance is by manipulating other people into their service. When all their intelligence and energy is directed toward manipulation children do not develop the perceptions and skills needed to become capable people. In his book *Raising Self-Reliant Children in a Self-Indulgent World* Dr. Stephen Glenn has identified the "significant seven" perceptions and skills necessary for developing capable people. They are:

1. Strong perceptions of personal capabilities ("I am capable.")

2. Strong perceptions of significance in primary relationships ("I contribute in meaningful ways and I am genuinely needed.")

3. Strong perceptions of personal power or influence over life ("I can influence what happens to me.")

4. Strong intrapersonal skills—the ability to understand personal emotions and to use that understanding to develop self-discipline and self-control.

5. Strong interpersonal skills—the ability to work with others and develop friendships through communication, cooperation, negotiation, sharing, empathizing, and listening.

6. Strong systemic skills—the ability to respond to the limits and consequences of everyday life with responsibility, adaptability, flexibility, and integrity.

7. Strong judgmental skills—the ability to use wisdom and to evaluate situations according to the appropriate values.

Most misbehavior can be traced to a lack of development in these significant seven perceptions and skills. Children developed these perceptions and skills naturally when they were allowed to work side by side with their parents, receiving on the job training while making meaningful contributions to the family lifestyle.

Today children do not have many natural opportunities to feel needed and significant but parents and teachers can thoughtfully provide these opportunities.

Understanding why children do not behave the way they used to is the first step for parents and teachers who are facing child-discipline problems. We need to understand why controlling methods, which worked so well when we were children, are not effective with children today. We need to understand our obligation to provide opportunities, which were once provided by circumstances, for children to develop responsibility and motivation. And most importantly, we need to know how to replace ineffective methods of dealing with our children with techniques that are effective with children today. The following chart explains the differences between the three main approaches for adult-child interaction.

STRICTNESS
(Excessive control)

· Order without freedom
· No choices
· "You do it because I said so."

PERMISSIVENESS   · Freedom without order
(No limits)   · Unlimited choices
                          · "You can do anything you
                            want."

POSITIVE DISCIPLINE   · Freedom with order
(Firmness with   · Limited choices
Dignity and Respect)   · "You can choose within
                            limits which show respect
                            for all."

Many adults refuse to give up their attempts to make
excessive control work because of their mistaken belief
that the only alternative is permissiveness—which is
much worse for children, and certainly worse for adults.
Children who are raised permissively grow up thinking
the world owes them a living. They are trained to use all
their energy and intelligence to manipulate and hassle
adults into taking care of their every wish. They spend
more time trying to get out of responsibility than developing their independence and capabilities.

Parents and teachers who don't like either method,
but don't know what else to do, may switch back and
forth in confusion between two ineffective alternatives.
They try excessive control until they can't stand themselves for sounding so tyrannical. They then switch to
permissiveness until they can't stand how spoiled and
demanding the children get—so they go back to excessive control.

If not strictness, and not permissiveness—then what?

Positive Discipline is an approach which is effective in
teaching children self-discipline, responsibility, cooperation, and problem-solving skills.

How is this different from other discipline methods? One difference is that *Positive Discipline is not humiliating to children, nor to adults.* Excessive control usually involves punishment which is humiliating to children. Permissiveness is humiliating to adults. Positive Discipline is based on mutual respect and cooperation. Positive Discipline incorporates firmness with dignity and respect.

Another difference is that *Positive Discipline teaches children self-discipline and responsibility.* When excessive control is used, it is the adult's responsibility to constantly be in charge of children's behavior. Adults must "catch" children being "good" so they can give rewards and "catch" them being "bad" so they can dole out punishment. Children do not learn to be responsible for their own behavior.

It is interesting to note how often controlling adults complain about irresponsibility in children without realizing they are training children to be irresponsible.

Permissiveness also teaches irresponsibility because adults and children both relinquish responsibility.

Many people feel strongly that strictness and punishment work. I agree. I would never say that punishment does not "work." Punishment does "work" in that it usually stops misbehavior immediately. But what are the long-range results? We are often fooled by immediate results. We forget to evaluate long-range results. Sometimes we must "beware of what works" when the long-range results are negative. The long-range results of punishment are that children feel one or all of the Four *R's of Punishment:*

1. *Resentment*—("This is unfair. I can't trust adults.")
2. *Revenge*—("They are winning now, but I'll get even.")

3. *Rebellion*—("I'll do just the opposite to prove I don't have to do it their way.")
4. *Retreat:*
   a. *Sneakiness*—("I won't get caught next time.")
   b. *Reduced self-esteem*—("I am a bad person.")

Children do not develop positive characteristics based on these feelings. Where did we ever get the crazy idea that in order to make children do better, first we have to make them feel worse? Think of the last time you felt humiliated or treated unfairly. Did you feel like cooperating or doing better?

What is the price when excessive control seems to work with some children? Research has shown that children who experience a great deal of punishment become either rebellious or fearfully submissive. The purpose of Positive Discipline is to achieve positive long-range results, as well as responsibility and cooperation now.

The *attitude* of a parent or teacher who has chosen each of the three approaches is very different.

Strictness—"These are the rules by which you must abide, and this is the punishment you will receive for violation of the rules." Children are not involved in the decision-making process.

Permissiveness—"There are no rules. I am sure we will love each other and be happy, and you will be able to choose your own rules later."

Positive Discipline—"Together we will decide on rules for our mutual benefit. We will also decide together on solutions that will be helpful to all concerned when we have problems. When I must use my judgement without your input, I will use firmness with dignity and respect."

As a fun way to illustrate the extreme differences between the three approaches, Dr. John Platt tells the story of three-year-old Johnny at breakfast time in each home.

In a strict home, where Mom knows what is best, Johnny does not have a choice regarding breakfast. On a cold, rainy day, controlling mothers all over the world know that Johnny needs some kind of hot mush to get him through the day. Johnny, however, has different ideas. He looks at the mush and says, "Yuk! I don't want this stuff!" One hundred years ago it was much easier to be a strict, controlling mother. She could just say, "Eat!" and Johnny would obey. It is more difficult today, so Mom goes through the following four steps in her effort to get obedience.

Step 1: Mom tries to convince Johnny why he needs hot mush to get him through the day. Remember what your mother told you hot mush would do inside your body? "It will stick to your ribs!" Have you ever thought about what a three-year-old thinks when he is told hot mush will stick to his ribs? He is not very impressed.

Step 2: Mom tries to make the mush taste better. She trys all kinds of concoctions—brown sugar, cinnamon, raisins, honey, maple syrup, and even chocolate chips. Johnny takes another bite and still says, "Yuk! I hate this stuff!"

Step 3: Mom tries to teach him a lesson in gratitude. "But Johnny, think of all the children in Africa who are starving to death." Johnny is still not impressed and replies, "Well, send it to them."

Step 4: Mom is now exasperated and feels her only alternative is to teach him a lesson for his disobedience. She gives him a spanking and tells him he can just be hungry.

Mom feels good about the way she handled the situation for about thirty minutes before she starts feeling guilty. What will people think when they find out she couldn't get her child to eat? And what if Johnny is really suffering from hunger? Johnny plays outside long enough to build up "guilt power" before he comes in and claims, "Mommy, my tummy is so hungry!" Mom now gets to give the most fun lecture of all—the "I told you so!" lecture. She doesn't notice that Johnny is staring into space while he waits for her to finish so he can get on with life. Mom feels very good about her lecture. She has now done her *duty* to let him know how *right* she was. She then gives him a cracker and sends him out to play again. To make up for the nutritional loss suffered from lack of a good breakfast, she goes into the kitchen and starts fixing liver and broccoli. Guess what lunch will be like?

The next scene takes place in a permissive home, where Mom is training a future anarchist of the world. When this Johnny comes into the kitchen, Mom says, "What would you like for breakfast, sweetheart?" Since Johnny has had three years of training, he is a *real* "sweetheart" and proceeds to run Mom through his training routine. Johnny first requests a soft-boiled egg on toast. He makes Mom cook nine eggs before she gets it just right. Then he decides he doesn't really want a soft-boiled egg, he wants French toast. Mom has three eggs left, so she whips up French toast. Meanwhile Johnny has been watching television. During the commercials he sees that athletes can do marvelous things if they eat "the Breakfast of Champions." He says, "I want Wheaties, Mom!" After he tastes the Wheaties, he changes his mind and asks for Sugar Crispies. Mom doesn't have Sugar Crispies, but runs to the store to get some. Johnny doesn't ever have to build up guilt power. He has Mom running on it twenty-four hours a day.

These stories are not exaggerations. They are examples of true situations. One mother told me her child wouldn't eat anything except potato chips. I asked her where he got them. She exclaimed, "Well, I buy them because he won't eat anything else!" Many children are being raised to be tyrants, who feel they are significant only if they can manipulate other people into fulfilling their demands.

We will now go into a home where Positive Discipline is used. There are two significant differences before breakfast starts. First, Johnny will be dressed and have his bed made before he even comes to breakfast. The second difference is that Johnny will do something to make a contribution to the family routine, such as setting the table, making the toast, or scrambling the eggs. (Yes, three-year-old children can scramble eggs, as you will see when we discuss chores.)

This morning is a cereal day. Mom gives Johnny a choice, "Would you like Cheerios or Wheaties?" (She doesn't buy sugar-coated cereals.) This Johnny has also been watching television commercials about what the great athletes eat, so he chooses Wheaties. After one taste, he changes his mind and says, "I don't want this stuff!" Mom says, "Fine. We can't recrisp the Wheaties. Go outside and play, and I'll see you at lunchtime." Notice that Mom skipped all the steps the controlling Mom went through. She didn't try to convince him or tell him about starving children or try to make it taste better. She didn't even have to spank him. She simply allowed him to experience the consequences of his choice.

Since Mom is new at this, Johnny tries to build up guilt power. Two hours later when he tells Mom that his tummy is so hungry, she respectfully replies, "I'll bet it is." Mom avoids her "I told you so" lecture and instead reassures Johnny, "I'm sure you can make it until lunch." It would be nice if the story could end here with understanding and cooperation from Johnny; however, it doesn't happen that quickly. Johnny is not used to Mom behaving this way. He is frustrated because he didn't get what he expected and has a temper tantrum. At this point it would be natural for most mothers to think, "This Positive Discipline stuff doesn't work." Johnny's Mom knew about the following illustration, which explains what often happens when we change our approach:

Children are used to getting certain responses from adults. When we change our responses, they will probably exaggerate their behavior (get worse) in their effort to get us to respond like we are supposed to. This is the kick-the-soda-machine effect. When we put money in the soda machine and a soda doesn't come out, we kick and pound to try and get it to do what it is "supposed" to do.

The problem with "Strictness" is that when misbehavior is met with punishment, the behavior stops immediately but soon begins again—and again and again.

Although misbehavior might get worse when Positive Discipline skills are first used, you will notice that there is a leveling off before the child misbehaves again. Misbehavior becomes less intense, with longer leveling-off periods, when the Positive Discipline is used consistently.

When we use firmness with dignity and respect, children soon learn that their misbehavior does not get the results they expect, and they are motivated to change their behavior. Once we realize this, going through the times when behavior gets worse for a short period is not as bad as the constant hassles of power struggles with an excessively controlling approach.

When Johnny has a temper tantrum, Mom can use the technique of a cooling-off period (explained later) and go to another room until they both feel better. It is not much fun to have a temper tantrum without an audience. They can then work on a solution to the problem together with mutual respect.

One of the most important concepts to understand about Positive Discipline is that children are more willing to follow rules that they have helped establish. They become effective decision makers with healthy self-concepts when they learn to be contributing members of a family and of society. These are important long-range effects of the Positive Approach.

Whenever parents and teachers are asked to make a list of characteristics they would like to help children develop, they think of the following qualities:

positive self-concept	interest in learning
responsibility	courtesy
self-discipline	honesty
cooperation	self-control
open-mindedness	patience
objective thinking skills	sense of humor
respect for self and others	concern for others
compassion	problem-solving skills
acceptance of self and others	inner wisdom
	enthusiasm for life
	integrity

Add any characteristics to the list that you feel have been left out. Keep these characteristics in mind as you study the concepts of Positive Discipline. It will be evident that children develop these characteristics when they are actively involved in this model of mutual respect and cooperation.

QUESTIONS FOR REVIEW OF CHAPTER 1

1. What are the two main reasons children don't behave the way they used to in the "good old days"?

2. Discuss the significant seven skills and perceptions and how a lack of these could lead to misbehavior in children.

3. What are three approaches to child discipline, and what are the differences between them?

4. Discuss the two main differences between Positive Discipline and other methods and why these differences are important for long-range results.

5. What is meant by "beware of what works"?

6. What are the Four R's of Punishment? Share personal experiences of times you felt any of the Four R's and why.

7. What are the long-range effects for children who learn through strict methods, and why?

8. What are the long-range effects for children who learn through Positive Discipline, and why?

9. Why do things sometimes get worse before they get better?

10. Discuss the characteristics you would like to see children internalize as a result of their interaction with you as a parent or teacher.

11. Why is it important to wait until you have more knowledge before you start discussing specific situations for problem solving? (See Introduction and Acknowledgments.)

Chapter Two

SOME BASIC CONCEPTS

Alfred Adler was a man with ideas ahead of his time. He was advocating equality for all people, all races, women, and children long before it was popular to do so. Adler, an Austrian of Jewish descent, had to leave his native land during the Nazi persecution in order to continue his work.

Rudolph Dreikurs worked closely with Adler and continued to develop Adlerian psychology after Adler's death in 1937. Dreikurs authored and coauthored many books (see "Suggested Reading") to help parents and teachers understand the practical application of Adlerian theory to improve their relationships with children at home and at school.

Before he died in 1971, Dreikurs was concerned because so many adults who attempted to practice his suggestions did not understand some of the basic concepts. This lack of understanding caused them to distort many of the techniques and use them to win over children rather than to win children over.

Winning over children makes them losers, and losing generally causes children to be rebellious or blindly submissive. Neither characteristic is desirable for children. Winning children over means gaining their cooperation in developing mutual respect, responsibility, self-discipline, and problem-solving skills.

An example of how adults misunderstand the basic concepts is the common practice of adding humiliation to a logical consequence because of the mistaken belief that children won't learn unless they *suffer* for their mistakes. *What* we do is never as important as *how* we do it. The feeling and attitude behind what we do will determine the "how." The feeling behind words is often most evident in our tone of voice. Adding humiliation violates the basic concept of mutual respect. It also changes what could be a logical consequence into punishment, which won't achieve positive long-range effects. If a child spills milk on the floor, the logical consequence would be for her to clean it up. It remains a logical consequence so long as the adult enforces this through kind but firm words, such as "Whoops, what do you need to do about that?" Another possibility is to respectfully say, "You'll need to clean that up before you pour some more." It becomes a punishment when a parent does not use a tone of voice that is kind and respectful or adds humiliation, such as, "How can you be so clumsy? Clean that up right now, and let me pour the milk from now on since you can't seem to get it right."

Adlerian psychology provides a set of basic concepts that offer a wealth of knowledge to help us increase our understanding of children and of ourselves, but it is so much more than just theory. The basic concepts are lost without attitudes of encouragement, understanding, and respect. If these attitudes are not understood, the techniques will be reduced to disrespectful manipulation.

Six basic Adlerian concepts are explained in this chapter so that practical application techniques can be properly understood. The explanations are oriented toward understanding children's behavior, but their application to adults will be obvious.

1. CHILDREN ARE SOCIAL BEINGS

Behavior is determined within a social context. Children make decisions about themselves and how to behave, based on how they see themselves in relationship to others and how they *think* others feel about them. This concept will make more sense when combined with the next two.

2. BEHAVIOR IS GOAL ORIENTED

Behavior is based on a goal to be achieved. Often children are not consciously aware of the goal they hope to achieve. Sometimes they have mistaken ideas of how to achieve what they want and behave in ways that achieve just the opposite of their goal. Dreikurs explained this when he said, "Children are good perceivers, but poor interpreters." Children are not the only ones with this problem, but the following situation is an example of how it begins.

When the mother of two-year-old Adele comes home

from the hospital with a new baby brother, Adele *perceives* how much attention Mother gives to the baby. Unfortunately, Adele *interprets* this to mean that Mother loves the baby more than her. This is not true, but the truth is not as important as what Adele *believes.* Her behavior will be based on what she believes is true rather than on what is true. Adele's goal is to regain her special place with Mother, and she mistakenly believes that the way to achieve this goal is to act like a baby. She achieves just the opposite of her goal by inspiring Mother to feel frustrated and rejecting rather than loving and affectionate.

3. A CHILD'S PRIMARY GOAL IS TO BELONG AND TO BE SIGNIFICANT

The first two concepts are brought together here as we see that the goal of all behavior is to achieve belonging and significance within the social environment.

Misbehavior is based on a mistaken belief about how to achieve belonging and significance, as in the foregoing example. This concept will be explained further in chapter 4.

4. A MISBEHAVING CHILD IS A DISCOURAGED CHILD

A misbehaving child is trying to tell us, "I don't feel I belong or have significance, and I have a mistaken belief about how to achieve it." Usually a misbehaving child acts obnoxious, so it is easy to understand why it is diffi-

cult for most adults to get past the misbehavior and remember the real meaning and message behind it. Hopefully this knowledge will help adults be more understanding and effective in helping misbehaving children.
Understanding is the first step. You will feel differently
about misbehavior if you remember that behind the misbehavior is a child who just wants to belong and is confused about how to accomplish this goal.

5. SOCIAL INTEREST

Another important contribution of Alfred Adler is the
concept of *Gemeinschaftsgefuehl,* a beautiful German word
coined by Adler. There is not a good English translation,
but Adler finally chose *social interest.* It means having real
concern for one's fellowperson and a sincere desire to
make a contribution to society. The following story was
shared by Kristin R. Pancer in the December 1978 issue
of the *Individual Psychologist* to convey the meaning of
social interest.

Once there were two brothers who owned a farm
together. They had a difficult time making a living because of the rocky soil and drought, but they shared all
profits equally. One of the brothers had a wife and five
children. The other was a bachelor. One night the married brother could not sleep. He tossed and turned as it
occurred to him how unfair their arrangement was. He
thought, "My brother does not have any children to go
home to, or to take care of him in his old age. He really
needs more than half. Tomorrow I will offer him two-
thirds of our profits. Surely that will be more equitable."
That same night the other brother also had difficulty

sleeping, because he also decided their fifty-fifty arrangement was not fair. He thought, "My brother has a wife and five children to feed. They also contribute more labor to the farm than I do. My brother deserves more than half. Tomorrow I will offer him two-thirds." The next day the brothers met and each shared his plan for a more equitable arrangement. This is an example of social interest in action.

Adler had what he called his *Fourteen-Day Cure Plan.* He claimed he could cure anyone of mental illness in just fourteen days if they would just do what he told them to do. One day a woman who was extremely depressed came to see Adler. He told her, "I can cure you of your depression in just fourteen days if you will follow my advice."

She was not very enthusiastic as she asked, "What do you want me to do?"

Adler replied, "If you will do one thing for someone else every day for fourteen days, at the end of that time your depression will be gone."

She objected, "Why should I do something for someone else, when no one ever does anything for me?"

Adler jokingly responded, "Well, maybe it will take you twenty-one days." He went on to add, "If you can't think of anything you are willing to do for someone else, just think of what you could do if you felt like it." Adler knew that if she would even think about doing something for someone else, she would be on her way toward improvement.

It is extremely important to teach social interest to children. What good is academic learning if young people do not learn to become contributing members of society? We have gone through an age of supermoms and superteachers, where children have learned to expect the world to serve them rather than to be of service to the world. These are the children who think it is unfair if they don't get their own way. When others refuse to serve them they feel sorry for themselves or seek revenge in some hurtful or destructive way. When they seek revenge, they always hurt themselves as much or more than they hurt others.

Positive Discipline helps children and adults end these vicious cycles by encouraging social interest.

6. EQUALITY

Many people today do not have trouble with the concept of equality until it comes to children. Then many objections are raised. "How can children be equal when they don't have the same experience, knowledge, or responsibility?" they ask.

Adler meant by equality that all people have equal claims to dignity and respect. Most adults are willing to agree that children are equal to them in value. This is one reason why this approach does not include humiliation. Humiliating techniques are contrary to the concepts of equality and mutual respect.

These six basic concepts provide the foundation for understanding behavior and developing the attitudes and techniques necessary to implement the Positive Discipline approach.

And there is one more key concept that unlocks all doors . . .

MAKE SURE THE MESSAGE OF LOVE GETS THROUGH

Mrs. Smith, a single parent, asked her parent study group for help with a problem she was having with her daughter, Maria. Mrs. Smith was afraid Maria might be getting into drugs. She had found a six-pack of beer on the floor in Maria's closet. She confronted Maria with the case of beer in her hand, "What is this!"

Maria replied, "It looks like a six-pack of beer to me, Mom."

Mrs. Smith said, "Don't get smart with me, young lady. You tell me about this."

Maria said, "Mom, I don't know what you are talking about!"

Mrs. Smith said, "I found this beer on the floor of your closet."

Maria remembered, "Oh, I forgot all about that. I was hiding that for a friend of mine."

Mrs. Smith sarcastically said, "Oh, sure! Do you think I'm going to believe that?"

Maria hostilely replied, "I don't care if you believe it or not," as she went into her bedroom and slammed the door.

Members of the group helped Mrs. Smith remember her bottom-line message of love by asking, "Why were you upset about finding the beer?"

Mrs. Smith indignantly replied, "Because I don't want her to get into trouble."

"Why don't you want her to get into trouble?" was the next question.

Mrs. Smith, feeling irritated by what seemed like stupid questions, answered, "Because I don't want her to ruin her life!"

The group members persisted, "Why don't you want her to ruin her life?"

"Because I love her!" Mrs. Smith exclaimed.

The final question was asked gently, "Do you think she got that message?"

Mrs. Smith felt chagrined as she realized she had not come even close to conveying her message of love to Maria.

The next week Mrs. Smith reported to her group how she had used Recovery and the Four Steps for Winning Cooperation. She said to Maria, "I'm really sorry for the way I blew up at you yesterday."

Maria said, "That's okay, Mom. I really was hiding it for a friend."

Mrs. Smith then shared, "Maria, I really do love you. I get scared sometimes that you might do things to ruin your life. I probably go overboard with my fears, and I forget to tell you that it is only because I love you."

Maria started to cry and said, "I have been feeling like I was just a big problem for you. At least my friends like me."

Mrs. Smith put her arms around Maria and said, "Will you give me another chance?"

Mrs. Smith reported that they started having family meetings that night. She felt grateful because an atmosphere of love and cooperation had been established which totally changed their relationship.

We experience so much more joy, as well as positive results, when we remember to make sure that the message of love gets through.

QUESTIONS FOR REVIEW OF CHAPTER 2

1. What is the difference between winning over the child and winning the child over?

2. What are the important attitudes necessary for the positive approach to be effective with children?

3. What does it mean to be a social being?

4. What is the primary goal toward which all behavior is oriented?

5. Why do children often behave in ways that are counterproductive to achieving their primary goal?

6. What is a misbehaving child trying to tell us with his or her misbehavior?

7. How might we behave differently if we remember the hidden message behind childrens' misbehavior?

8. What is social interest and why is it important for children to develop it?

9. What does Adler mean by equality?

10. Why is humiliation out of place in a positive approach?

11. What is the key concept that unlocks all doors? Share an example of how something you did with a child might have been different if you had started with the message of love.

Chapter Three

THE SIGNIFICANCE OF BIRTH ORDER

The purpose of learning about the significance of the birth order is to increase our understanding of how children might develop misperceptions about themselves based on their interpretations of their position in the family. It is another way of "getting into the child's world" in order to increase our understanding of their reality.

It is very common for children to compare themselves to their siblings and assume that if a brother or sister is doing well in a certain area their only choice is one of the following:

- to develop competence in a completely different area
- to compete to try to be "better than"
- to be rebellious or revengeful
- to give up

Being in a family is like being in a play. Each birth-order position is like a different *part* in the play, with distinct and separate characteristics for each part. There-fore, if one sibling has already filled a part, such as the *good* child, other siblings may feel they have to find other parts to play, such as rebellious child, academic child, athletic child, social child, and so on.

All oldest children will not be exactly alike, nor will all middle children, all only children, or all youngest children be exactly alike. We are all unique and have as many differences as we do similarities, but those of the same birth order often adopt similar characteristics.

It seems more logical for children to have similarities because they come from the same family than because they come from the same birth order, but the opposite is true. Children in the same family are often extremely different, even though they have the same parents, the same home, and the same neighborhood. Of course, the environment cannot be totally the same for children in the same family, but the factor which makes the biggest contribution to differences within families is the *interpre-tation* each child gives to the environment he *perceives*.

As we saw in the previous chapter, children are *good perceivers* but *poor interpreters*. This becomes very apparent in the study of birth order. The truth of a situation is not as important as the interpretation of a situation. Behavior is based on the latter. Children of the same birth order often make similar interpretations about themselves and how they think they need to behave in order to find belonging and significance in life.

Other basic concepts discussed in the previous chapter are also consequential in studying the significance of birth order. Children make interpretations about themselves as social beings within their family constellation, and also adopt mistaken beliefs about how to find belonging and significance, because of their birth order.

The purpose for learning about birth order is not to label and stereotype. It is rather to help us increase our knowledge and understanding of ourselves and of children so we can become more effective in our relationships.

The most predictable similarities are found among oldest children, because this is the one position that has the fewest variables. For instance, there are many ways to be a middle child, such as the middle of three or one of the middles of seven. Youngest children have almost as many predictable similarities as do oldest children. Only children will be more similar to oldest or youngest, depending on whether they were pampered like the youngest or given more responsibility like an oldest.

Before you read further, close your eyes and think of several adjectives that come to your mind to describe the oldest, youngest, and middle children you know. We will discuss the similarities first, then the variables that account for uniqueness, and finally the exceptions to the general rules.

It is easy to come up with descriptions of oldest children, such as responsible, leader, bossy (even though in their minds they want others to do better for their own good), perfectionist, critical (of self and others), conformist, organized, competitive, independent, reluctant risk-takers, and conservative. Because oldest children are the first born, they often adopt the mistaken interpretation that they must be first or best in order to be important. This can be manifested in many different ways. For some it may seem important to get their school work done first, even though it is sloppy. Others may be the last one to hand in their work because they take so much time making it the best.

The characteristic we think of first to describe youngest children is spoiled. Many youngest children are pampered, both by parents and by other siblings. This makes it very easy for them to adopt the mistaken interpretation that they must continue to manipulate others into their service in order to be important. Youngest are often skilled in using their charm to inspire others to do things for them. Youngest children are also creative and fun-loving. Much of their energy and intelligence is channeled into achieving significance through manipulation.

Often youngest are put in the confusing position of being favored by parents and resented by their siblings. The greatest danger for children who have been pampered is that they often interpret life as unfair whenever they are not taken care of or given whatever they want. They often feel hurt by these unfair conditions and think they have a right to have temper tantrums, feel sorry for themselves, or seek revenge in some way that is destructive or hurtful to others.

Youngest children may also have difficulty adjusting to school. They may feel not only that the teacher should continue the service they have received at home, but that the teacher should also learn for them. Consciously they say, "Teacher, please tie my shoes for me." Subconsciously, and by their actions, they are saying, "And while you are at it, please learn for me." "I can't," and "show me," are often simple demands to "do it for me."

As an elementary school counselor, I have talked with many children who have difficulty adjusting to the learning environment. I always ask these children, "Who dresses you in the morning?" As you might guess, there is usually someone else who is still taking the responsibility to dress them. Children can dress themselves very well from the time they are two years old if they have clothes that are easy to put on and have been taught how to do it. When parents continue to dress their children after the age of two, they are robbing them of responsibility, self-sufficiency, and self-confidence. Without these skills, they will not be good learners in school.

Since pampering is so damaging to children, why do parents do it? Many parents really think it is the best way to show love to their children. I have heard some argue that children have plenty of time to adjust to the cold, cruel world; so why not let them have it easy and pleasurable for as long as possible? These parents are not aware of how difficult it is to change habits and characteristics once they are established. Other reasons parents might pamper are because it is easier, it fills their needs to be needed, they think that is what "good" parents are supposed to do, they want to be sure their children do not experience the difficult childhood they feel they had, or they feel pressure from friends and family.

Adlerians have a great interest in destroying the myth that "supermoms" are good for children. It is important to educate parents on what a great disservice they do their children when they pamper them. Dreikurs said, "Never do anything for a child that the child can do for himself." Take time for training, and then allow children to develop responsibility and self-confidence. It is a mistake to think children can always learn to take care of themselves later. The longer they wait, the more difficult it is to change their interpretations of *how life is* and what they think they need to do to find belonging and significance.

Many youngest children choose an entirely different interpretation of life and become speeders. They often adopt the mistaken interpretation that they must catch up with and outdo everyone ahead of them in order to be important. They become adults who are overachievers still trying to prove their significance.

It is more difficult to generalize about characteristics of middle children because of the many different positions. They usually feel squeezed in the middle, without the privileges of the oldest or the benefits of the youngest. This provides good reason to adopt the mistaken interpretation that they must be different in some way in order to be significant. This difference may take the form of overachieving or underachieving, "social butterfly" or "shy wallflower," "rebel with a cause" or just plain "rebel." Many are more easygoing than their siblings. Most middle children have a great deal of empathy for the underdog, with whom they identify. They are often good peacemakers, and others seek them out for sympathy and understanding.

As explained earlier, only children may be similar to oldest or youngest children, with some important differences. If they are like the oldest, it will be with less intensity for perfectionism, because they haven't felt the pressure from someone coming up behind them to threaten their position. However, lessened perfectionism does not remove this trait entirely. Only children usually have the same high expectations of themselves that they felt from their parents. Because they have been the only child in the family, they usually desire and appreciate solitude—or they may fear loneliness. It is more important for them to be unique than first.

All of the original astronauts were either oldest, psychological oldest, or only children. Neil Armstrong, an only child, had the unique experience of being the first man to walk on the moon.

How does birth-order information help us to understand children and be more effective with them? Being aware of a child's birth order will allow us to make some intelligent guesses about the child's world and point of view. Hopefully this awareness will help parents and teachers understand the importance of avoiding pampering, of providing oldest children with opportunities to feel okay about losing and not always being first, of helping middle children feel less squeezed, and generally of getting into each child's world.

Mark is an oldest child who could not stand to lose at games by the time he was eight years old. Dad was contributing to Mark's attitude by always letting him win at chess, because he didn't like to see Mark get upset and cry. After learning about birth order, Dad realized it was more important to allow Mark some experience with losing, so he started winning at least half the games. Mark was upset at first, but soon began to win and lose with more grace. Dad felt a milestone had been reached one day when he was playing catch with Mark and threw a bad ball. Instead of getting upset about missing the ball, Mark was able to use his sense of humor and commented, "Nice throw, Dad. Lousy catch, Mark."

There are many factors that explain exceptions to general rules. One is gender. If the first and second child are different sexes, they may both develop characteristics of an oldest child, especially if there is a definite division of sex roles in their family. Each will assume oldest-child responsibilities within their sex role. For instance, if the oldest is a boy, he will have oldest-child characteristics in the masculine role. If the second child is a girl, she will still develop oldest-child characteristics in the female role.

However, if the two oldest children of three or more siblings are of the same sex, the differences between the two are likely to be extreme. The two oldest children are usually complete opposites. The closer they are in age, the more pronounced the differences, which brings us to the second factor accounting for exceptions to general rules.

When there are four years or more between children, they are less influenced by each other. If there are five children in a family with more than four years between each child, each will develop characteristics closer to an only or oldest child. In a family where there are seven children ages nineteen, seventeen, fifteen, nine, seven, three, and one, there will be one actual oldest. The children who are nine and three will be *psychologically oldest* children, because the sibling before them is four or more years older. There will also be one actual youngest and two *psychological youngest*—the children who are fifteen and seven—because they were youngest children for four or more years before the next sibling was born. When a child has had an opportunity to be in a position for more than four years, he has already formed many interpretations about life and himself and how to find belonging and significance. These may be modified when the family constellation changes but usually are not changed entirely.

Another exception to the rule is that children sometimes arbitrarily switch typical position characteristics. A second child may become an "Avis" child—one who *tries harder* and overtakes the first. The oldest may then *give up* and relinquish the typical characteristics of a first child. A sure sign of perfectionism is giving up if you can't be the best or first.

A youngest who becomes a speeder leaves the role of the pampered vacant. Usually the child who is second from the youngest will move in to fill this role and adopt characteristics of a youngest.

Another factor that accounts for exceptions to the general rule is the family atmosphere. This can either increase or decrease differences. In families where competition is valued and modeled (as in many American families), differences will be increased. In families where cooperation is valued and modeled, differences will be decreased.

As stated earlier, one general rule that can almost always be counted on is that the two oldest children will be very different from each other if they are the same sex and close in age. While doing an Adlerian Life-style Interview with one lady who had a sister only eighteen months older, my first guess was that they would be extreme opposites in characteristics. The interview proved this guess to be wrong. They were very similar. When we came to the question regarding what her parents were like, I asked if I could guess before she told me. I guessed that her parents were very loving and cooperative with each other, they agreed on childrearing techniques, and the children felt they were loved and treated fairly. She asked me how I knew. I based my guess on my knowledge of the effects of family atmosphere.

Since two sisters only eighteen months apart were similar in characteristics, instead of opposites, we can guess that the parents created an atmosphere of cooperation rather than competition.

Remember, this information is not to be used to increase our feelings of superiority, so we can feel smug about being "right" about others. It is not to be used to stereotype and label. It is simply to aid us in understanding why children often have mistaken interpretations about how to find belonging and significance, so we can be aware of more effective ways to help (or know when we should refrain from helping). It can also be used to focus on strengths.

We should always remember to look for and appreciate the many ways each individual is unique.

In one school district this information was used for staff members to become aware of the high number of youngest or psychologically youngest children in educationally handicapped classes. This raised a valid question about educational handicaps. Are they physiological or behavioral? If they are physiological, are we missing many educational handicaps in older children because they learn to overcompensate? Do youngest children learn to *use* handicaps to obtain more special service?

In one elementary school, a group of students seemed to be driving every teacher crazy. When this group was in the second grade, their teacher thought of retiring. When they were in the third grade, their teacher could hardly wait for summer. Finally, the fourth-grade teacher took a birth-order survey and learned that 85 percent were youngest children. Many of them spent a great deal of time displaying helplessness and seeking special attention. Through the use of class meetings, the fourth-grade teacher was able to achieve significant improvement as the children learned to help each other and themselves through problem-solving skills.

Judy Moore, a fifth-grade teacher did her master's

thesis on birth order and reading groups. She found there was a high percentage of oldest and only children in top reading groups and youngest children in lowest reading groups. Mrs. Moore took tape recordings of the dynamics in each group while she asked questions. In the top group all the children would raise their hands in eager competition to be the first to answer. The middle group was more easygoing, but someone would usually have an answer. In the lowest group there was a greater tendency for the children to express lack of understanding and need for further help.

Mrs. Moore had one student in her class (I'll call him John) who was her very lowest reader. She was concerned about the possibility of mental retardation, so her first step toward helping was to request psychological testing. She then did a Life-style Interview with John and learned that he was the youngest. Even more interesting, he had three older sisters with names like Georgia, Roberta, and Paula. She learned that everyone in the family called John "King John." With this information, Mrs. Moore could make some educated guesses about the value of boys in this family and the possibility of extreme pampering. Why should John want to do anything for himself, including learning, if he had never had much experience with responsibility? Mrs. Moore's hunches were confirmed when she received the report from the psychologist that John was gifted. He had been using all his intelligence to sharpen his charming manipulation skills.

Mrs. Moore kindly confronted John and told him she now knew he was a very capable young man who could do well in a top reading group. She moved him to a top group, and he lived up to her expectations. The biggest problem was for John's sisters, who thought Mrs. Moore was being unreasonable to expect and insist on so much from their little brother.

It would be devastating to tell most oldest children they could do better if they tried. The reason an oldest might not be doing as well as possible is that trying too hard for perfection often causes this child to be too tense to perform well.

It might be discouraging to tell a middle child he could do better if he tried because of his mistaken interpretation that he cannot do as well as older siblings who already have that area all "sewed" up.

Youngest children often do not like being told they could do better because of their mistaken interpretation that they have more belonging and significance when others are taking care of them, but it can be effective, as in the case of John.

Knowledge of birth order can help you as a parent or teacher get into the child's world. Just letting another person know that you can see, understand, and respect his or her point of view is one of the most encouraging things you can do. To be able to say, "I can understand how you must feel" is quite different from the accusation and blame of "Well, no wonder you act that way, since you are an oldest (middle, youngest, only)."

It is interesting to contemplate the implications of birth-order information as it relates to marriage. As you might guess, there is often an attraction between oldest and youngest children. Youngest like to be taken care of, oldest like to take care of, so it seems like a perfect match. However, as Adler said, "Tell me your complaint about your spouse and I will tell you why you married that person in the first place." The very characteristics that attract in the beginning often irritate later. In this case the oldest may later get tired of always being the responsible partner and may criticize their more irresponsible spouse, forgetting that this very trait seemed attractive in the beginning. The youngest may also get tired of being taken care of and told what to do—except when they decide they want it. The problem is that when they want it is often not when the oldest wants to give it.

When two oldest children marry because of admiration for the traits they also respect in themselves, the trouble begins when they can't agree on who is in charge or who really knows the *best* way to do things.

Two youngest may marry because they recognize how much fun they can have together, but later may resent the other for not taking better care of them.

It may be easiest or hardest for middles to adjust to any situation, depending on how rebellious or easygoing they have become.

All combinations can be successful with understanding, mutual respect, cooperation, and a good sense of humor. A good friend of mine is a youngest married to a youngest. They started off on a vacation. He turned to her and asked if she had made motel reservations. She replied, "No, didn't you?" They both laughed and had a good time finding a motel.

Teaching styles may vary because of birth order. Teachers who are oldest children often like to be in charge. They are often willing to organize interesting and complicated projects for their students to be involved in. They prefer structure and order and are happiest when children are sitting in neat rows doing as they have been told. Since this scene is not as typical as it used to be, many of these teachers are frustrated, until they learn methods to help them achieve order without being authoritarian. They are quick to see the long-range benefits of a positive approach for children and for themselves.

Teachers who are middle children are often as interested in the psychological well-being of their students as they are in academic achievement. They are drawn to the rebellious students and hope to influence them in a more positive direction. These teachers try to achieve order through mutual respect and understanding.

Teachers who are youngest children are often creative and fun-loving and have the easiest time adjusting to noise and disorder. These teachers are often willing to allow children to take more responsibility so that they won't have to do everything themselves.

The following exercise is an excellent way to experience the similarities and differences of people in the same birth-order position.

Group Exercise (Felt tip-pens and butcher paper are needed.)

Instructions for Group Leader

Have the group divide into smaller groups of the same birth-order position. First give them the following instructions: "Each member of the group think of adjectives that describe you as a person. Suggest these adjectives to your group. If the majority agrees that characteristic fits them also, write it down on the butcher paper."

Allow about ten minutes for this exercise and then have each group use masking tape to hang their butcher paper on the wall. You can then have a discussion about how well their findings match the information given in this chapter on birth order. Be sure to discuss the following points:

· Factors that account for exceptions and uniqueness
· The importance of stressing the positive traits of each birth-order position
· Ways in which the information can be used to increase understanding of children and ourselves
· The destructiveness of using this to label or stereotype

Also, ask the group if anyone gained insight about why he might have formed certain interpretations regarding himself and mistaken beliefs about what he needs to do to find belonging and significance.

QUESTIONS FOR REVIEW OF CHAPTER 3

1. Discuss the main purpose of understanding birth order and how it might help us in working with children.

2. What are some common choices children make when they compare themselves to their siblings?

3. What are some ways we can misuse knowledge about birth order?

4. List the typical characteristics of each birth order position.

5. Discuss the dangers of pampering and why some parents do it.

6. Discuss the factors that account for exceptions to general rules about birth order.

Chapter Four

FOUR MISTAKEN GOALS OF BEHAVIOR

When Rudolph Dreikurs explained the four mistaken goals, people often asked, "How can you keep putting children in these boxes?"

He would reply, "I don't keep putting them there, I keep finding them there." As he studied children's behavior, Dreikurs discovered four inappropriate or *mistaken* goals children adopt as a rationale for misbehaving.

The four mistaken goals of behavior are:

1. *Attention* (I belong only when I have your attention.)

2. *Power* (I belong only when I'm winning, or at least when I don't let you win.)

3. *Revenge* (It hurts that I don't belong, but at least I can hurt back.)

4. *Assumed inadequacy* (I give up. It is impossible to belong.)

The true primary goal of all behavior is to find a sense of belonging and significance. Children (and many adults) adopt one or more of these four mistaken goals because they believe that:

· *Attention* or *power* will help them achieve belonging and significance.
· *Revenge* will give some satisfaction for the hurt experienced in not feeling a sense of belonging and significance.
· *Assumed inadequacy* will help them avoid the hurt of even trying to achieve what they mistakenly believe is not possible.

Why is it important to identify the mistaken goal? We need to know the goal being used so that we can know the most effective action we can take to help children.

Identifying the mistaken goal is not always easy, because a child may use the same misbehavior to achieve any of the four mistaken goals. For example, a child may refuse to do his work in order to gain attention, to show power, to seek revenge, or to display inadequacy. Understanding the goal is important in knowing what to do.

For each mistaken goal, the child's mistaken belief will be different, as follows:

Attention: I feel a sense of belonging and significance only if I receive constant attention and keep you busy with me.

Power: I feel a sense of belonging and significance only if I am the boss and do what I want to do.

Revenge: I feel hurt because I do not have a sense of belonging and significance, so I have a right to hurt others as I have been hurt.

Assumed inadequacy: I do not feel it is possible for me to belong and have significance, so I will give up and hope that people will leave me alone.

Children are not aware of their mistaken belief. If you ask them why they misbehave, they will tell you they don't know or will give some other excuse. Later I will explain how you can use *goal disclosure* to help the child become aware of his or her mistaken goal.

There are two clues adults can use to help them identify the mistaken goal.

Clue Number 1: The adult's feeling reaction to the misbehavior.

When asked for their feeling reaction to misbehavior, many adults respond with the words *anger* or *frustration,* which are both secondary responses to a primary feeling reaction. The primary reactions experienced when encountering a child misbehaving at one of the four mistaken goals are those of feeling irritated, annoyed, threatened, hurt, or inadequate. Feeling threatened, hurt, or inadequate are such helpless feelings that we quickly cover them with the secondary response of anger. With anger we at least have a sense of *pseudo* power—we can do *something,* even though that "something" is merely to rant and rave or lash out. Frustration and anger are both secondary responses to being unable to control the situation that causes our more primary feelings.

When trying to identify your feeling reaction to misbehavior, dig down to the primary feelings. The primary feeling reaction adults experience when confronted with misbehavior for each of the four mistaken goals is as follows:

If you are feeling irritation or annoyance, the child's goal is likely to be *attention.*

If you are feeling threatened (you want to be the boss as much as the child does), the child's goal is likely to be *power.* If you react with power, you will become involved in a power struggle.

If you are feeling hurt (how could the child do such a thing when you try so hard to be a good parent or teacher?), the child's goal is likely to be *revenge.* If you cover your primary feeling with anger, you will become involved in a revenge cycle.

If you are feeling inadequate (how can I possibly reach and inspire this child?), the child's goal is likely to be *assumed inadequacy.* If you give in to your feeling, you will be giving up just as the child has.

Clue Number 2: *The child's response when you tell him or her to stop the misbehavior.*

Attention: The child stops for a while, but usually soon resumes the same behavior or some other behavior to get your attention.

Power: The child continues misbehaving and may verbally defy or passively resist your request to stop. This often escalates to a power struggle between you and the child.

Revenge: The child retaliates by doing something destructive or saying something hurtful. This often escalates to a revenge cycle between you and the child.

Assumed inadequacy: The child is passive, hoping you will soon give up and leave him alone.

EFFECTIVE REMEDIES FOR EACH MISTAKEN GOAL

There is never just one way to solve behavior problems. Certain corrective methods are more acceptable to some parents and teachers than to others. Group members can give several possible suggestions based on the principles you will learn in this book. The parent or teacher seeking help can then choose the most acceptable suggestion.

Most problems can best be solved in a family or class meeting, but there are alternative techniques when more immediate action is desired or necessary. The following general guidelines for effective responses to each mistaken goal are discussed in more detail in later chapters. They are outlined here to emphasize how many different solutions there are to any problem or goal of misbehavior.

After you have read the entire book and understand the techniques of Positive Discipline, you may want to refer back to this outline as a reminder of effective methods for each goal. The basic attitudes of encouragement, understanding, and mutual respect, as discussed in previous chapters, are the keys to success.

Attention:

· Ignore the misbehavior, but give attention during pleasant times.
· Redirect the child into contributing behavior.
· Impose a logical consequence.
· Give a choice.
· Do the unexpected.
· Set up a schedule for spending special time with the child on a regular basis.

Power:

· Withdraw from the power struggle to allow for a cooling-off period, then do one of the following:

· Use the four steps for winning cooperation.

· Follow up with a one-to-one problem-solving session.

· Redirect the child to use power constructively.

· Shut your mouth and act—kindly, but firmly.

· Decide what you will do, not what you will try to make the child do.

· Set up a schedule for spending special time with the child on a regular basis.

Revenge:

· Withdraw from the revenge cycle by avoiding retaliation.

· Remain friendly while waiting for the cooling-off period.

· Win cooperation.

· Cooperate in one-to-one problem solving.

· Use encouragement.

· Set up a schedule for spending special time with the child on a regular basis.

Assumed Inadequacy:

· Take time for training.

· Arrange for small successes.

· Use encouragement.

· Do not give up.

· Spend regular, special time with the child.

To emphasize that the same behavior could represent all four mistaken goals, we will go back to the example of the child who will not do his work.

If the child's goal is **attention,** you feel annoyed. When you tell the child to do his work, he will do it for a while. To help this child you might simply ignore his unfinished work and show appreciation in areas where he cooperates. This allows him to learn that not doing his work is not a good way to get attention. You could give him a choice about when he wants to do it—now or after school. You could redirect his misbehavior by asking him to help you with some task as soon as he is finished with his work. Or you could tell him you will wink at him and smile every time you see he is not doing his work. It is especially effective if you make this arrangement with him after you have done goal disclosure, which will be explained later. It may seem that winking and smiling will reinforce his bid for attention by not doing his work, but instead it helps the child feel belonging and significance so that he soon does not feel the need to get attention in this way.

If the child's goal is **power,** you feel your power is threatened and will want to show her you can make her do it. When you tell this child to do her work, she will tell you she won't or will passively ignore you. If you insist on winning by imposing some punishment, she may shift to the goal of revenge. The way to help this child is to wait until you are no longer feeling the urge to *make* her do it.

Children who are into power are usually involved with an adult who is into power. It is the adult's responsibility to change this atmosphere. When you truly want mutual respect and cooperation based on mutual understanding and shared decision making, children will know the difference. When they trust this difference, they will cooperate.

During a one-to-one problem-solving discussion, admit that you have been participating in a power struggle. State that you would really like to change your relationship with the child and start solving problems with mutual respect and understanding. Tell her you would like her help in letting you know whenever she feels you are trying to overpower or manipulate her. Share your willingness to work together toward solutions that would satisfy both of you. Remember that children are more willing to follow solutions when they have been involved in the decision.

Family meetings and class meetings are very effective in solving power issues.

Children who are into power often have good leadership qualities. You could let this child know you appreciate these qualities and ask for help in some leadership task. One teacher trained children to be peer counselors (see appendix) to help other children with playground problems.

Teachers may simply *act* by giving the child a poor grade for unfinished work. An attitude of kindness and firmness is important.

If the child's goal is **revenge,** you feel hurt. You can't understand why the child won't do his work when you have tried so hard as a parent or teacher. When you tell this child to do his work, he may say something hurtful, such as "I hate you." Or he may do something destructive, such as tearing up his paper.

To help this child, do not retaliate. Remain friendly by saying, "I can see that you are upset, so we can't discuss

this now, but I would like to talk to you later." After a
cooling-off period you can use the *Four Steps for Winning
Cooperation* or you can ignore the problem and share
special interests, as described in chapter 6.

If the child's goal is **assumed inadequacy,** you may
feel inadequate about helping her. When you ask her to
do her work, she looks dejected and hopes you will soon
leave her alone. To help this child, be sure she knows
how to do the work. Take time for training, even if you
feel the child should understand because you have already explained it many times. The difference between
a child who won't do her work in order to gain attention
and the child who won't do her work because of assumed
inadequacy is that the former really does know how to
do it and is just trying to manipulate you into helping
because of the mistaken belief that she doesn't "belong"
unless you are paying attention to her. The latter is more
severely discouraged because she really does not think
she can do it and does not want your attention. Since the
behavior can be similar for children in these two goals,
it is important to sharpen your awareness so that you can
feel when a child is simply trying to keep you busy with
her or when a child would really prefer that you stay
away from her.

Another possibility is to ask this child if she would
like your help or if she would like to choose another
student to help her. Or, you might try finding a level
where she does feel adequate and let her work at that
level. Be sure to arrange the situation so that she will
be successful.

Don't give up. This child may do some work just to
get you off her back. Whatever the reason, if she does
some work, she will have some success and feel en-

couraged. Spending special time with this child is very important.

GOAL DISCLOSURE

Children are not aware of their mistaken goal. Goal disclosure is one way to help them become aware of their mistaken belief.

Goal disclosure should be conducted by teachers or counselors. It is essential to be objective and friendly during the process. It is almost impossible for parents to be objective with their own children, so it does not seem to work for them.

Since objectivity and friendliness are essential, goal disclosure should not be done at the time of conflict. It is best to talk to the child alone when you are learning this procedure. Trained counselors can do goal disclosure in groups or in front of an audience.

First you ask the child if she knows why she is misbehaving. You should name the misbehavior specifically, such as, "Mary, do you know why you keep wandering around the room when you are supposed to be in your seat?"

Children will usually say, "I don't know." It is true that they don't know. Even if they give some reason, it is not the *real* reason. If they give a reason, you say, "I have some other ideas. Would it be okay with you if I guess? You can tell me if I'm right or wrong."

If they say they don't know, just ask if you can guess. If your manner is objective and friendly, the child will be intrigued and anxious to have you guess. You then ask what Dreikurs called the "could it be"

questions as follows, waiting for the child to respond
to each question.

"Could it be that the reason you wander around the
room is to get my attention and keep me busy with you?"
(Attention)

"Could it be that the reason you wander around the
room is to show me you can do whatever you want?"
(Power)

"Could it be that the reason you wander around the
room is because you feel hurt and want to get even with
me or someone else?" (Revenge)

"Could it be that you wander around the room because you don't feel you can succeed so you don't even
want to try?" (Assumed Inadequacy)

There are two responses that will let you know if your
guess is correct and the child has become aware of her
goal. The first is a *recognition reflex*. This means that the
child will involuntarily smile. Sometimes this smile will
be accompanied with the answer no. The recognition
reflex tells you your guess is right even though the child
denies it. The other response is a simple yes. Once you
have a recognition reflex or an affirmative response,
there is no need to go on to the other questions.

Goal disclosure can be your third clue to identifying
the mistaken goal. There is a film of Dreikurs interview-
ing a child when he seems certain that the child's goal is
power. He keeps trying to get a recognition reflex by
asking the "could it be" question in many different ways
to indicate power, but continuously gets a negative response and no recognition reflex. Dreikurs finally goes
on to ask the question indicating revenge, and the child
agrees that is it.

Teachers can use goal disclosure to increase their understanding and to show interest in the child. Once you know the goal, you can use it as a basis for discussion and problem solving. If the goal is attention, you can explain to the child that everyone wants attention. You can then redirect the child into constructive ways of seeking attention. You could also agree to give the child attention for her misbehavior and let her know you will wink and smile to let her know she has your attention an agreed-upon number of times. Make this a special conspiracy between the two of you.

If the goal is power, you can admit that you are powerless to force her to behave differently. You can then ask for her cooperation in designing a plan of mutual respect and cooperation.

If the goal is revenge, you can show your interest in understanding what you or someone else might have done to hurt her. Caring enough to listen without judgment can be the most encouraging procedure for this goal. After the child feels understood, she will be more willing to hear your point of view and then work on solutions.

If the goal is assumed inadequacy, tell the child you can understand how she might feel because you feel discouraged yourself sometimes. This should be followed by expressions of faith in her ability and a plan to ensure success.

Degree of Discouragement

The goal the child chooses indicates the degree of discouragement. The mistaken goal of attention shows the least discouragement, and assumed inadequacy shows the most serious discouragement.

Children do not necessarily start with the first goal of attention and work their way down through assumed inadequacy. Children who are more passive might go directly to assumed inadequacy if treated harshly or for some other reason believe they lack belonging and significance.

Children who are spunky enough to choose power might never go to assumed inadequacy, but they are often pushed to revenge by adults who insist on winning the power struggle.

Mrs. Smith shared why she was so grateful to learn about the four mistaken goals and corrective remedies. Her oldest child, Billy, was an extremely difficult child. He was always doing hurtful or destructive things, as in the following example.

One day the whole Smith family (Mr. and Mrs. Smith, Billy, his younger brother, Brad, and baby Maria) spent the day looking at properties. Billy and Brad complained constantly about how bored and hot they were. They kept requesting to go home. Two-year-old Maria was content, napping on Mother's lap when she got tired.

The Smiths wanted to continue their search for property the next day, but decided to do Billy and Brad a favor by leaving them home with a neighbor. It was a nice day, and they were old enough to play with their friends in the neighborhood. Since Maria had not been any trouble and was too young to play in the neighborhood, they decided to take her with them. When they got ready to go, Billy said he wanted to go. Mrs. Smith reminded him how hot and bored he had been and tried to convince him he would be happier staying home. Billy insisted he wanted to go. Mrs. Smith was firm in her decision and even gave Billy and Brad a quarter for popsicles as a treat (bribe). Billy was still not satisfied, but they left him anyway.

When they came home, Mrs. Smith was dismayed to see that Billy had taken a knife and slashed the Naugahyde on Maria's highchair. Mrs. Smith's first reaction was to feel hurt as she wondered, "How could he do such a thing?" She quickly covered her hurt with anger, spanked Billy, and sent him to his room.

At the time this incident occurred, Mrs. Smith was also attending a parent study group and keeping a journal to remind her of situations she would like to work on with the group. As soon as she started writing in her journal, she was able to be objective enough to see things from Billy's point of view and she understood why his mistaken goal was revenge. She used the Four Steps for Winning Cooperation (explained in the next chapter) as follows:

Mrs. Smith went into Billy's room and asked, "Did you think the reason we wanted to take Maria and not you is because we loved her more than you?" Billy tearfully replied yes.

Mrs. Smith said, "I can understand how it might seem that way to you. I'll bet that didn't make you feel very good." Billy started to cry.

Mrs. Smith put her arms around him and waited for him to stop crying. She then said, "I think I can understand what you felt. When I was thirteen, my mother took my sixteen-year-old sister to New York City. I wanted to go but was told I was too young. I didn't believe that. I really thought it was because my mother loved my sister more than me." Billy was very sympathetic. Mrs. Smith then asked Billy, "Would you like to know how I felt?" Billy nodded. Mrs. Smith told him, "I felt bad yesterday because you were so hot and bored. It was not very enjoyable for us to look at property when you were so miserable. I really thought we would all be happier if you stayed home to play with your friends so you wouldn't be bored. Can you understand why I thought I was doing you a favor?"

Billy said, "I guess so."

Mrs. Smith added, "I can see why you might have thought we loved Maria more, since we took her and not you, but that is not true. I love you very much. I would have preferred to leave Maria home too, but I knew she couldn't go out and play with her friends the way you could."

Mrs. Smith continued to hold Billy for a while and then asked, "What do you think we should do to fix the highchair?"

Billy said with enthusiasm, "I can fix it."

Mrs. Smith said, "I'll bet you can."

They worked out a plan to use some of his allowance to buy a piece of Naugahyde, cut out a pattern and together stapled it to the chair. The highchair was better than before—and so was their relationship.

Mrs. Smith realized that she and Billy had been engaging in a revenge cycle. He had adopted the mistaken belief that he was not loved (lacked belonging and significance). This hurt and inspired the mistaken goal of wanting to hurt back. Billy would do something hurtful or destructive, but Mrs. Smith tended to cover her hurt with anger and would retaliate against Billy with more punishment. They were engaged in a revenge cycle.

Mrs. Smith realized now that the chair was already damaged and that punishment would not fix it. She also knew she couldn't ignore such behavior. Punishment gave her the feeling that she had not let him "get away with it," but she now understood that it did not produce the long-range goals she wanted.

After realizing Billy's mistaken goal of revenge, Mrs. Smith was able to handle it effectively to produce long-range results. When Billy would do something destructive, she would acknowledge that she could see he was hurt and upset, and they would talk about it later. After a cooling-off period she would go through the four steps for winning cooperation, as she did in the above example, and they would end up with a solution that brought them closer together, rather than continuing the revenge cycle.

This all happened five years ago. Mrs. Smith reports that she and Billy now have an excellent relationship. Billy is seldom hurtful or destructive anymore. She hates to think of how things would be if they had continued their revenge cycle.

The above story is an example of the *Four Steps for Winning Cooperation,* which is explained in chapter 6, and also illustrates how mistakes can be opportunities to learn and improve.

WORKING WITH TEENAGERS

As you look at the four mistaken goals of behavior, I am sure you will recognize that even adults often adopt these mistaken goals and beliefs. However, it is not quite so simple to find children in one of these four "boxes" after they reach the age of eleven or twelve.

Many misbehaving teenagers have the mistaken goal of power or revenge, but other factors are involved, too.

Peer pressure is extremely important to teenagers. Younger children are influenced by peer pressure, but adult approval is even more important to them. For this reason peer pressure can be used to encourage young children to seek adult approval. Peer approval is more important to teenagers than adult approval and becomes one of their mistaken goals.

Teenagers also have the mistaken goal of excitement. They often do things "just for the fun of it"—even though it may be destructive or hurtful to others. Children who have this goal have not learned social interest. Fortunately, many teenagers do not experience this goal, and most of those who do give it up as they become adults.

Excessively controlling methods can be disastrous with teenagers, who are usually even less willing than younger children to assume an inferior, submissive position. When teenagers have been subjected to controlling behavior from adults, they are very suspicious of the word *cooperation.* They interpret it to mean "give in!" They are often right—that is what many adults mean by cooperation.

The only way to win the cooperation of teenagers is through mutual respect and equality in problem solving. Family meetings and class meetings teach social interest and get children involved in the decision-making process. When they are involved, they cooperate.

SUMMARY

The four goals discussed in this chapter are called mistaken goals because they lead to misbehavior due to mistaken beliefs about how to find belonging and significance. The four mistaken goals represent four mistaken beliefs children adopt when they feel they do not have belonging and significance.

A misbehaving child is a discouraged child. The discouragement comes from beliefs and feelings of not belonging or not having significance. It does not matter whether the beliefs are based on facts or imagination. Behavior is based on what the child thinks is true, not what is true.

Sometimes it is difficult for us, as parents and teachers, to remember that misbehaving children are trying to tell us they want to belong when their behavior inspires frustration rather than love and caring. Some experts believe we will reinforce the misbehavior if we respond positively to a child who is misbehaving. If, however, we understand that a misbehaving child is a discouraged child, it is obvious that the best way to remove the motivation for misbehavior is to find a positive way to help the child feel belonging and significance.

Accepting this concept intellectually is one thing, but it is quite another to put it into practice for two reasons:

1. Most adults do not feel like being positive when a child is misbehaving.

2. The rare adult who is able to react to misbehavior with positive encouragement will often be rejected by the child. This is because children (like most of us) are not receptive to encouragement when they need it the most. They are too emotionally upset to accept it. Wait for a *cooling-off period* and try again with encouragement.

The child who needs love the most is often the child who is the most unlovable.

MISTAKEN-GOAL CHART

Mistaken Belief	Adult's Feeling	Child's Response	Mistaken Goal	Corrective Measures (Choose one or more.)
I belong only when I have constant attention.	Annoyed. Desire to remind or coax.	Child stops temporarily when attention given.	Attention	Ignore the behavior. Redirect behavior. Logical consequences. Give choice. Do the unexpected. Encourage.
I belong only when I am in power or winning or am not allowing you to win.	Provoked, threatened, challenged: "I'll make you do it!"	Intensifies misbehavior with passive or aggressive defiance.	Power	Withdraw from power struggle. Wait for cooling-off period. Win child over for problem solving. Act. Decide what you will do. Encourage.
I can't belong, but I can hurt others back.	Hurt (covered by anger) "How could you do this to me when I try to do so much for you?"	Retaliates with more hurtful or destructive behavior.	Revenge	Withdraw from revenge cycle for friendly cooling-off period. Win child over. Use encouragement and problem solving.
It is not possible to belong. I give up.	Inadequate to help. Pity for child.	Passive. Avoids attention.	Assumed inadequacy	Avoid pity. Take time for training and encouragement. Arrange for small successes. Don't give up.

Adapted from an original chart by Nancy Pearcy and Louise Van Vliet.

Understanding the four mistaken goals of behavior helps adults remember what children are really saying with their misbehavior. "I just want to belong." It also helps us know what to do to help resolve the problem when immediate encouragement is not effective because of emotional involvement.

Remember that understanding the four goals and learning what to do for more immediate results will not solve the problem permanently. Only helping the child feel belonging and significance through encouragement will have long-range effects. If encouragement cannot be given or accepted at the time of the problem behavior, it should always be considered essential as a follow-up after a *cooling-off period.* Also, keep in mind that it takes two for a power struggle or a revenge cycle. You might want to take a look at your own mistaken goals and work on changing them for more democratic attitudes and behavior.

QUESTIONS FOR REVIEW OF CHAPTER 4

1. What are the four mistaken goals of behavior?
2. What is the child's mistaken belief for each goal?
3. Why is it important to identify the goal?
4. What are the two clues that help adults identify the goal?
5. What is the adult's primary feeling reaction to behavior in response to each of the four goals? (Answer this question for each goal, one at a time.)
6. How do children respond when misbehaving within each of the four goals when you tell them to stop their misbehavior? (Answer for each goal.)

7. What are some effective responses or actions adults can take to help correct the misbehavior at each goal? (These methods are explained in greater detail in later chapters.)

8. Why are the four goals called mistaken goals?

9. Children do not base their behavior on what is *true* but rather on what?

10. What is a child trying to tell with his misbehavior?

11. Why is it difficult to remember what the child is trying to tell us?

12. Why might children reject our attempts to be positive when they are misbehaving?

13. What kind of child usually needs love the most?

14. What is the most important thing we can do to help a child overcome his or her motivation to misbehave?

Chapter Five

NATURAL AND LOGICAL CONSEQUENCES

Have you ever wondered what children are thinking about when they are being punished? Many are thinking about revenge. Punished children often do something to get even very soon. After children experience punishment, they are usually left with a sense of unfairness. Instead of focusing on the behavior that inspired the punishment, they focus on anger toward the adult who imposed the punishment.

Some adults make the mistake of thinking that children continue to misbehave because the punishment wasn't severe enough to teach them a lesson. So they punish again, more severely—and children find more clever ways to get even. A revenge cycle is perpetuated. Parents may not recognize the severity of the revenge cycle until their child is a teenager and rebels totally by running away, getting involved in the drug scene, getting pregnant, or some other extremely hurtful event.

The irony is that the child hurts himself through revenge as much or more than he hurts his parents.

Other children, while being punished, are making a vow not to get caught next time. Some children decide not to repeat the behavior that caused the punishment; but they do so because of fear and intimidation, not because they have developed principles regarding right and wrong.

I am not saying that punishment does not work. Anyone who has been involved with children knows they will stop misbehaving when punished, at least for a while. For this reason adults may think they are winning many discipline battles. However, they have inevitably lost the discipline war when children are inspired to get even, avoid detection, or conform out of fear.

Again, we must beware of what "works" and consider the long-range results. As long as it is important for adults to *win,* they are trying to make *losers* out of children.

To end the discipline war, it is imperative to stay out of power struggles and create an atmosphere where the long-range effects for both children and adults are mutual respect, responsibility, self-discipline, and cooperation in solving problems.

Adults must take the leadership role by using techniques that inspire a positive atmosphere for winning children over rather than winning over children. One of these techniques is the use of natural and logical consequences instead of punishment.

What are the natural and logical consequences and how do they differ from punishment?

A *natural* consequence is anything that happens *naturally,* with *no adult interference.* When you stand in the rain, you get wet. When you don't eat, you get hungry. When you forget your coat, you get cold. *Logical* consequences, on the other hand, *require the intervention of an adult,* or other children in a family meeting or a class meeting. Children can learn a great deal from natural and logical consequences to help them develop responsibility. Let's look first at an example of how natural consequences work.

Billy, a first-grader, forgot his lunch every day. Mother would interrupt her busy schedule to drive to school with his lunch. After learning about natural consequences, she decided that Billy would probably learn to remember his lunch if he had to do without it for a day or so. She first discussed this with Billy, letting him know she was confident that he could be responsible for remembering his lunch. She also told him she would no longer bring his lunch to school if he forgot it because she knew he could learn from mistakes.

Her intentions were sabotaged for a while because Billy's teacher took over and loaned him money for lunch when he forgot. It was not until Mother and Billy's teacher got together on a plan to allow Billy to learn from the natural consequences of his behavior that he became responsible for remembering his lunch.

Billy tested the plan. The first time he forgot his lunch, he asked his teacher if he could borrow some lunch money. She said, "I'm sorry, Billy, but we agreed that you could handle your lunch problem by yourself." Billy then phoned his mother and demanded that she bring his lunch. She also kindly but firmly reminded him that he could be responsible. Billy pouted for a while, even though one of his friends gave him half a sandwich.

After that, Billy seldom forgot his lunch. When he did

forget it, he managed to find someone who would share some food with him. By the time Billy reached the second grade, he added the responsibility of making his own lunch, as well as remembering to take it.

Natural consequences were effective in helping eleven-year-old Julie be responsible for her own clean clothes. Mother was constantly nagging Julie to put her dirty clothes in the hamper. Julie did not respond to the nagging, but constantly complained because the clothes she wanted to wear were not clean. Mother would often give in and hurriedly do a special wash when Julie complained.

Mother decided to try natural consequences. She kindly but firmly told Julie she had confidence in her ability to be responsible for her clothes. She explained that from now on she would wash only the clothes that were in the hamper on wash days. She would allow Julie to experience the natural consequences of not having her clothes in the hamper before washtime.

Julie also tested this plan. A few days later she wanted to wear some pants which she had neglected to put in the hamper to be washed. When Julie complained, Mother empathetically said, "I'll bet you are really disappointed that they are not clean." When Julie pleaded with her to do a special wash, Mother said, "I'm sure you can figure out another solution." She then got into the shower to avoid further discussion during this time of conflict. Julie was upset that she had to wear something else that day, but it was a long time before she forgot to put her clothes in the hamper.

Even though natural consequences are often the best way to help a child learn the results of behavior, there are times when natural consequences are not practical:

· *When a child is in danger.* Adults cannot allow a child to experience the natural consequences of playing in the street, for example.

When this point is made, someone inevitably uses it as a reason for spanking, using the argument, "I have to spank my child to teach her not to run in the street." I ask this parent if she would be willing to let her unsupervised toddler play near a busy street after she has been spanked to "teach" her to stay out of the street. The reply is always negative. I then ask when she would feel it is safe to let her child play unsupervised near a busy street. Most parents agree that they would not let their children play unsupervised near a busy street until they are somewhere between five and eight years of age, no matter how many spankings they have had to "teach" them to stay out of the street. This illustrates the fact that maturity, or readiness to learn certain responsibilities, is more important than spankings.

Adults still need to take time for training while children are maturing, but it is more effective and less humiliating to use logical consequences to help children develop responsibility. The logical consequence in this case would be to put the child in the house or backyard every time she runs into the street. She will actually learn more from this than from a spanking, but will still not be ready for unsupervised play until she is older.

· *When natural consequences interfere with the rights of others.* Adults cannot allow the natural consequences of allowing a child to throw rocks at another person, for example.

· *When the results of children's behavior do not seem like a problem to them,* natural consequences are ineffective. For example, it does not seem like a problem to some children if they don't take a bath, don't brush their teeth, don't do their homework, and eat tons of junkfood.

We should switch to logical consequences to help children learn responsible cooperation when their behavior causes problems for others or potential danger and when it doesn't seem like a problem to them. As noted earlier, logical consequences are different from natural consequences, in that they require the intervention of an adult, or other children in a family meeting or a class meeting to help children experience consequences for misbehavior. For example:

Linda liked to tap her pencil while doing desk work. This disturbed the other children. Her teacher gave her the choice to stop tapping or to give up her pencil and complete the work later. (It is usually a good idea to *give children a choice* either to stop their misbehavior or to experience the logical consequence.)

Dan brought a toy car to school. His teacher called him aside and asked him if he would like to leave it with her or with the principal until after school. Dan chose to leave it with his teacher. (It is a good idea to speak to children about a consequence in private, when possible, so they don't lose face with their peers.)

Giving children a choice and speaking to them in private about the consequences are not the only guidelines for effective logical consequences. If this were so, it would be reasonable to give a child a choice, in private, either to stop his misbehavior or to have a spanking.

Rudolph Dreikurs was very concerned when he saw many parents and teachers using punishment and calling it the Dreikurs method of logical consequences.

The Three Rs for Logical Consequences is a formula

that identifies the criteria to ensure that solutions are logical consequences, rather than punishment. They are:

1. Related
2. Respectful
3. Reasonable

If any of the Three Rs is missing from a solution, it can no longer be called a logical consequence.

When a child writes on a desk, it is easy to conclude that the *related* consequence would be to have the child clean up the desk. But what happens if either of the other two Rs is missing?

If a teacher is not *respectful* and adds humiliation to his request that the desk be cleaned, it is no longer a logical consequence. Mr. Martin thought he was using a logical consequence when he said to Mary in front of the whole class, "Mary, I'm surprised that you would do such a stupid thing. Now clean up that desk or I'll have to let your parents know how disappointed I am in you." In this example, respect has been eliminated and humiliation substituted.

If a teacher is not *reasonable* and requests that a student clean every desk in the room to make sure she has learned her lesson, it is no longer a logical consequence. Reasonableness has been eliminated in the favor of the power to ensure suffering. This is usually because of the mistaken belief that children learn only if they suffer.

When a child spills milk, the related consequence is to have him clean up the spill. It is not respectful if you say, "How can you be so clumsy? That is the last time I'll let you pour milk." A more respectful comment would be, "Whoops. What do you need to do?" If the child doesn't know what to do, it is because you haven't taken time for training. Handling it this way also demonstrates that mistakes are wonderful opportunities to learn. It would not be reasonable to ensure that he suffers for his mistake by saying, "To make sure you learn, I want you to scrub the whole floor."

Actually, if adults eliminate one of the Three Rs so that consequences are not *related, respectful, and reasonable,* children will experience the Three Rs of Punishment, first explained in chapter 1. They are repeated again here:

1. Resentment (This is unfair. I can't trust adults.")
2. Revenge ("They are winning now, but I'll get even.")
3. Retreat, in the form of rebellion ("I won't get caught next time.") or reduced self-esteem ("I am a bad person.")

Parents and teachers don't like to admit that, often, the main reason they like to use punishment is to demonstrate their power to win over the child or to gain revenge by making the child suffer. The subconscious thinking behind this idea is, "I am the adult and you are the child. You will do what I say—or else you will pay."

This concept was depicted in a cartoon showing a mother watching her husband chase their child with a stick. In the caption the mother is calling, "Wait, give him another chance." The father replies, "But he might not ever do it again."

Obviously, it is more important for this father (and many adults) to make the child suffer for his misbehavior than to help him change it.

Suffering is not a requirement of logical consequences. For example, a child might enjoy being sent to his room where he can play with his toys or read. (This is fine, since the purpose of the isolation is to stop the misbehavior, not to get revenge by causing suffering.)

Isolation can be a solution that meets the criteria of the Three Rs of Logical Consequences when used with the following guidelines:

· Take time for training. Talk about how helpful isolation can be before you use it. Teach children about the value of a cooling-off period and the importance of waiting until everyone feels better before trying to solve conflicts.

· Develop a plan in advance that you may need to go to your room or your child may need to go to his room. Explain that the purpose of isolation is not to punish or to suffer. Give suggestions of things the child could do to encourage himself to feel better while in his room, such as reading, playing with toys, resting, or listening to music.

· Finally, the suggestion for isolation should be followed with the encouraging statement that the child may return whenever he feels ready.

These guidelines for isolation are equally appropriate for teachers, who should have a time-out area for children. The only difference would be in the suggestions of things to do to feel better, such as resting, doing their work without interruption, or thinking about possible solutions.

Martha sent her child to his room because he was misbehaving. When he came out of his room a few min-

utes later, she sent him right back. When asked if her
child was still misbehaving when he came out of his
room, she admitted he wasn't. She grinned as she realized it would not have been necessary to send him back
to his room if she had kept in mind her goal of changing
his behavior rather than her power to ensure suffering.

Where did we ever get the crazy idea that in order to
make children perform better, we must first make them
feel worse?

This power to impose suffering is a common mistake
made by many parents and teachers—so much so that
they often lose sight of their primary goal of inspiring
children to improve their behavior.

Once parents and teachers become convinced of the
value of natural and logical consequences, they can still
be very difficult to use. Our only training for parenting
has been the model our parents gave us, which often did
not include natural and logical consequences.

Parents and teachers also don't like to admit that punishment can feel good to them because it gives them that
sense of power they feel is being taken away from them
when children misbehave. This, of course, is not part of
their conscious awareness, but when confronted with it
they usually recognize it.

In rational moments, adults know that their bottom-
line goal is to inspire children to be happy, responsible
people. However, it is so easy to get lost in pride and ego
goals.

Ineffective behavior on the part of adults is not always
based on pride and ego. Sometimes they are honestly
misguided. Many believe that punishment is the best way
to motivate children to do better. They really believe that
in order to make children do better, they first have to
make them feel worse.

Mark was being very disrespectful and disruptive in class by talking when the teacher was trying to teach. Mr. Smith, his teacher, punished him by telling him he had to write thirty sentences, "I will use the proper manners and will not be disrespectful while in a classroom." Unfortunately Mark did not think, "Oh great! I really deserve this, and it will teach me not to talk in class anymore." Instead he felt rebellious and resentful. So he didn't write the sentences. Mr. Smith agrees with many adults who think that if the punishment doesn't work, it is only because it was not severe enough—so Mr. Smith doubled the "sentence" to sixty sentences.

Mark felt even more resentful and rebellious and refused to do it. His mother pointed out that if he didn't do it, they would probably be doubled again (whether it was fair or not) and that he would probably be suspended. Mark said, "I don't care, I'm not doing it." The "sentence" was doubled again to 120 sentences, and Mother was called in for a conference. Many teachers also believe that if the punishment is not working, it is because the parents aren't supporting the punishment. Mark's mother was a leader of parent study groups and did not believe in the effectiveness of punishment.

At the conference, she established that she certainly agreed that Mark had been disrespectful and disruptive and that this should be corrected. She made the suggestion, "Since Mark did something to make your job unpleasant, how about having him do something to make up for it that would help make your job be more pleasant?

Mr. Smith said, "Like what?"

She suggested cleaning the blackboards, emptying the trash, or teaching part of a lesson.

Mark was really interested in this suggestion and

chimed in, "Yeah, I could teach about transitives and intransitives."

Mr. Smith said, "Yes, you did understand that, and many of the students haven't grasped it yet." He then looked at Mark's mother and stated, "But he would enjoy that."

Mr. Smith was not willing to follow the suggestion to redirect misbehavior into contributing behavior because he was afraid that would be rewarding misbehavior and would inspire Mark to continue misbehaving.

This is an excellent example of the misconception that in order to make children do better, we first have to make them feel worse. Many teachers, as you will see in later examples, have found that redirecting misbehavior into contributing behavior has worked to encourage children to stop, or greatly diminish, their misbehavior.

Another reason logical consequences can be difficult to use is that it takes thought, patience, and self-control. Many adults find it easier to request this of children than to do it themselves.

Dreikurs taught the importance of being both kind and firm in our relations with children. Kindness is important in order to show respect for the child. Firmness is important in order to show respect for ourselves and for the needs of the situation. Authoritarian procedures usually lack kindness. Permissive procedures lack firmness. Kindness and firmness are essential for a positive approach.

Dreikurs also recognized that some people find it easy to be firm but not to be kind. They prefer authoritarian methods. Others find it easy to be kind but not to be firm. They usually fall into permissiveness. The majority of us can be both kind and firm, but not at the same time, especially when confronted with a misbehaving child.

When I first learned about these concepts, I felt it was important to be open, honest, and spontaneous. My problem was that the open, honest, spontaneous reaction to my misbehaving children was threatening, yelling, and spanking. I knew it would not be honest or spontaneous to act kind when I felt the need to be firm, since I was usually angry over the misbehavior. However, I reasoned with myself that it was not too much to ask that I control my behavior, since that is what I was expecting of my children. It took practice, but the results were worth the effort.

My first experience with logical consequences failed because I had missed the importance of being both kind and firm and I did not know about the Three Rs for Logical Consequences. I was firm, but not kind, and added humiliation.

I told my children in advance that if they were late for dinner, they would have to go without food until breakfast. I did not want to take the responsibility of finding them or of cooking and cleaning up twice. The first time they were late, instead of being kind and firm in carrying out this decision, I scolded them for not remembering and added my "I told you so's." I turned what could have been a logical consequence into punishment, and then wondered why it wasn't effective.

Later, I was successful in using logical consequences because I had learned all the guidelines. For years I had been nagging my children about getting dressed in the morning. After learning the concepts of natural and logical consequences, we had a family meeting and together decided that breakfast would be served from eight to eight-thirty in the morning. Anyone who was not dressed and ready to eat by then would have to wait for lunch to eat. Because the children had been involved in the decision, they seemed eager to cooperate for the first few weeks. Seven-year-old Kenny even decided to arrange his clothes fireman-style so that he could get dressed quickly in the morning.

Kenny was also the first one to test the plan. One morning he sat on the couch in his pajamas with one eye on the clock. At 8:31 A.M. he came into the kitchen and demanded his breakfast. I said, "Sorry, Kenny, but breakfast is over. I'm sure you can make it until lunch." Kenny argued that he wasn't going to wait and climbed up on the counter to get some cereal. I had to grit my teeth to remain *kind* while I *firmly* lifted him down from the counter. He cried and had a first-class temper tantrum for about forty-five minutes, stopping only long enough to try getting up on the counter once in a while. Each time, I kindly and firmly lifted him down. He finally went outside. I wasn't at all sure that it had worked and remembered how much easier it was to punish instead of going through that for forty-five minutes.

For the next two weeks, everyone was dressed and ready for breakfast on time. Then Kenny decided to test the rule once more. When he came to the table in his pajamas at 8:31, I repeated what I had said the last time, "I'm sorry you missed breakfast. I'm sure you can make it until lunch." I was thinking, "Oh no. I don't think I can take another forty-five minutes of kindness and firmness while he has a temper tantrum."

To my delight, I had to lift him down from the counter only once before he mumbled under his breath as he went out to play, "I didn't want any breakfast anyway."

That was the last time I had a problem with the children getting dressed in the morning before breakfast. It had worked!

This example is an illustration of two other concepts discussed earlier:

1. Things usually get worse before they get better as children test the plan. It is difficult but effective to remain kind and firm during this testing period.

2. Punishment may get quicker results, but logical consequences help children develop the characteristics necessary for long-range results.

Janet liked to dawdle and seldom finished her schoolwork during the time allotted in class. Her teacher finally told Janet that any work not finished before recess would have to be done at the work bench during recess. She spent two days at the work bench during recess before she decided to get her work done on time.

There is never just one possible logical consequence for a problem situation. There are several possible variations in solving the preceding problem.

Some teachers do not like to have children miss recess and would prefer to have them stay after school to complete their work. In some schools the teachers have made arrangements for students who haven't completed work on time to take their work into another class that isn't having recess at the time. These students are respectfully required to sit at the back of the room and do their work.

If teachers are concerned about children not getting enough exercise, they might require that the student do twenty-five jumping jacks before taking their work to another class or to sit on the work bench. This is not punishment as long as the Three Rs for Logical Consequences are remembered.

Following is an example where either a natural or a

logical consequence would have been effective, but neither was used.

Gina lost her softball mitt. The natural consequence would have been for her to do without. However, mother is such a supermom that she can't stand having her "poor darling" suffer in this way. After giving Gina a moralizing lecture (one Gina has heard many times) about how she should take care of her things, Mother drove her to the store (as usual, promising she would never do this again) to purchase another mitt. Not allowing Gina to experience the natural consequence would not have been so bad if mother had substituted the logical consequence of having Gina earn the money to pay for a new mitt. But Gina's mother is like so many others. Her intervention did not resemble logic.

Gina has been well trained to know that she does not have to be the responsible one, even if she does make a big fuss about it.

Many parents and teachers use the phrase "I've told you a hundred times." They need to realize that it is not the children who are dense. Children know what works for them. Adults need to learn that telling a hundred times is not effective. Children will never learn to be responsible for their own behavior as long as adults take that responsibility away from them by repeating reminders or by solving problems *for* them, rather than *with* them.

Mrs. Silvester had told her children a hundred times to pick up their toys. After learning these concepts she kindly let her children know that from now on if they didn't pick up their toys, she would. She added, however, that if she picked them up, she would put each one away until they could demonstrate that they would take care of them by picking up their other toys.

Keep in mind that, often, the problem of toys being left out is a problem of too many toys having been purchased by parents. When this is the case, children don't care if you do pick them up and put them away permanently. These parents should "own" the problem and do something about it, rather than expecting cooperation from their children.

Mrs. Silvester learned which toys her children really cared about and which ones were a result of her problem of buying too many toys. When toys were left out, she would say only once, "Do you want to pick up your toys or do you want me to?" Her children picked up the ones they cared about. The ones she picked up stayed on her top shelf and were forgotten.

When all the toys the children did not want had been put up, Mrs. Silvester told her children she would no longer warn them, but would just pick up any toys that had not been put away. She did not have to pick up many toys. When her children asked for toys she had put away, she would give them back only after they had kept their toys picked up for a week.

Mrs. Silvester added a sequel to this story. The only toys she buys now are those the children want badly enough to save their allowance until they can pay at least half. She no longer has a serious problem.

It takes practice to become proficient at using natural and logical consequences. I remember what the process was like for me. First, I would remember (after I was all through with my usual, ineffective way of handling things) that I should have used a logical consequence—but I didn't know what a good consequence would have been. Later, I progressed and knew (when I was in the middle of doing my usual thing) that I should be using a logical consequence—but still didn't know what a good consequence would be. Then I would remember (before starting my usual habits) that it would be a good idea to use a logical consequence—but I still couldn't think quickly enough to come up with a good one.

It was while I was hesitating, trying to think of a logical consequence that I learned the value of doing nothing. I would emotionally withdraw while I was thinking and either the children would solve their own problem or the atmosphere would change simply because I wasn't getting involved.

This leads to another guideline to remember: Logical consequences are not the best solution for every problem. Many parents and teachers get so excited about logical consequences that they try to find a consequence for every misbehavior.

Logical consequences are effective at the time of conflict only if the goal is attention. When the goal is power or revenge, logical consequences can be effective during a problem-solving session *after* a cooling-off period, and *after* winning the child's cooperation.

Natural and logical consequences should *not* be used when the mistaken goal is assumed inadequacy.

I found it helpful to keep a journal. I started recording all the problem situations I encountered. By the time I started writing, I had calmed down sufficiently to be more objective and was able to understand the dynamics of the problems more thoroughly. I could then identify the mistaken goal, so I would know which solutions would be the most effective. I also found I could think of logical consequences when I wasn't emotionally involved. Most problems are repeated, so I would be ready with a consequence the next time—if I had determined that a logical consequence would be the most effective procedure to solve the problem.

Parents and teachers who are just beginning to use these techniques should work on only one thing at a time and remember to have the courage to be imperfect. Eventually, you will realize that the use of natural and logical consequences is an important technique in helping children develop the long-range characteristics of self-discipline, responsibility, cooperation, and problem-solving skills.

Natural and logical consequences are effective for long-range results, because, after children experience them, they are left with a sense of fairness, even though they may not have liked the consequences. Instead of focusing on anger at adults and desire for revenge, they are able to focus on their behavior and to use their energy to realize logical reasons for cooperation and responsibility. These children learn to be contributing members of society, which greatly enhances their self-esteem and sense of belonging and significance.

QUESTIONS FOR REVIEW OF CHAPTER 5

1. What are many children thinking about while they are being punished?

2. What are the immediate results of punishment?

3. What are the long-range results of punishment?

4. Why must we sometimes beware of what works?

5. If adults insist on winning, what position does that leave for children?

6. What is the definition of a natural consequence? Give some examples.

7. What part do adults play in natural consequences?

8. What is the definition of a logical consequence?

9. What are the three Rs for logical consequences?

10. Give an example of how a logical consequence becomes a punishment if any one of the three Rs is missing.

11. When children don't experience the three Rs for logical consequences, what are the other three Rs they may experience?

12. What is the mistaken belief of adults when they use their power to ensure suffering?

13. What guidelines should be followed when using isolation?

14. Why is it important to be both kind and firm at the same time

15. Why is it difficult to be both kind and firm at the same time?

16. Why is doing nothing sometimes the most effective thing you can do?

17. Are logical consequences the best solution for every misbehavior problem?

18. For which mistaken goal are logical consequences usually effective, even during the time of conflict?

19. What are the two things that must take place before logical consequences can be used during a problem-solving session when the mistaken goal is power or revenge?

20. For which mistaken goal should natural and logical consequences not be used?

21. Why are natural and logical consequences effective in helping children develop long-range positive characteristics?

Chapter Six

USING ENCOURAGEMENT EFFECTIVELY

If a child came up to you and innocently said, "I am a child, and I just want to belong," could you get angry and put that child down in any way? Of course not! What most adults don't realize is that any child who is misbehaving is subconsciously saying, "I just want to belong, and I have some mistaken ideas about how to accomplish belonging."

A misbehaving child is a discouraged child, and we are more effective in redirecting the misbehavior to positive behavior when we remember the hidden message behind the behavior. The misbehaving child is letting us know he does not think he has belonging and significance, and he has mistaken beliefs about how to find belonging and significance.

Accepting this premise, it is obvious that the best way to help a misbehaving child is through encouragement. When discouragement is removed, the motivation for misbehavior will be gone also.

Dreikurs emphasizes encouragement and feels it is the most important skill adults can learn in helping children. He said many times, "Children need encouragement, just as plants need water. They cannot survive without it."

Not too long ago, my son had been whining and I was so annoyed I felt like spanking him. Instead, remembering this concept, I knelt down, gave him a hug, and told him how much I loved him. Not only did he stop whining and crying, but my annoyance "magically" disappeared when I remembered the hidden message behind his behavior and took a few minutes to do something encouraging, rather than punishing.

Unfortunately, encouragement is not always so simple as the previous example might indicate. In this chapter we will explore several ways of increasing our understanding of encouragement and how to use it effectively to help children.

TIMING

In the foregoing example, my son responded favorably to encouragement while he was misbehaving. Usually encouragement is favorably received only after a *cooling-off period*. At the time of conflict, especially if the mistaken goal is power or revenge, both adult and child are feeling too angry to be able to give or receive encouragement. For this reason, friendly withdrawal is often the most effective thing to do at the time of conflict. If you can't simply walk away or ignore the conflict-causing behavior until you both have a chance to cool off, at least use "I" messages to express your feelings and intentions, rather than hurtful comments or blame.

Mr. Anderson shared this experience in a parent study group. He told his eight-year-old son, "I'm so angry right now, you had better run or I might hit you." So his son ran. They then solved the problem after they had both cooled off.

Teachers can withdraw by stating, "I think we are both too upset to discuss this now, but I would like to get together with you when we have both had time to cool off." This is especially effective if you have discussed the concept of a cooling-off period during a class meeting.

If you do not have success with encouragement, it could be that your timing is off. Recognizing the importance of a cooling-off period will increase your success ratio.

WINNING COOPERATION

Children feel encouraged when they think you understand their point of view. Once they feel understood, they are more willing to listen to your point of view and to work on a solution to the problem.

Using the following "Four Steps for Winning Cooperation" is a great way to create an atmosphere where children are ready for cooperation.

1. Express understanding for how you think the child might be feeling. Be sure to check with him to see if you are right.

2. Show understanding. Understanding does not mean you agree or condone. It simply means you understand the child's perception. A nice touch here is to share times when you have felt or behaved similarly.

3. Share your feelings and perceptions. If the first two steps have been done in a sincere and friendly manner, the child will be ready to listen to you.

4. Ask if the child would be willing to work on a solution with you. Ask if he has any ideas on what to do in the future to avoid the problem. If he doesn't, offer some suggestions and seek his agreement.

An attitude of friendliness, caring, and respect are basic to these steps. Your decision to use these steps will be enough to create positive feelings in you. After the first two steps, the child will be won over, too. He will now be ready to hear you when you use the third step (even though you may have expressed your feelings many times before without being heard.) The fourth step is for solutions—which will work now that you have created an atmosphere of respect.

Mrs. Martinez shared the following experience. Her daughter, Linda, came home from school complaining that her teacher had yelled at her in front of the whole class. Mrs. Martinez put her hands on her hips and asked Linda in an accusing voice, "What did you do?"

Linda dropped her eyes and angrily replied, "I didn't do anything."

Mrs. Martinez said, "Oh, come on, teachers don't yell at students for nothing." Linda flopped on the couch with a sullen look on her face and just glared at her mother. Mrs. Martinez continued with her accusing tone, "Well, what are you going to do to solve this problem?"

Linda belligerently replied, "Nothing."

At this point Mrs. Martinez remembered the concept of winning cooperation. She changed her attitude and commented in a friendly tone of voice, "I'll bet you felt embarrassed to have the teacher yell at you in front of others." Linda looked up at her mother with suspicious interest. Mrs. Martinez then shared, "I can remember once that happened to me when I was in the fourth grade, because I got up to sharpen my pencil during a math test. I was embarrassed and angry that my teacher would yell at me in front of the whole class."

Linda was really interested now. "Really?" she said, "All I did was ask to borrow a pencil. I certainly didn't think it was fair for my teacher to yell at me for that."

Mrs. Martinez said, "Well, I can certainly understand how you must have felt. Can you think of anything you might do to avoid that kind of embarrassing situation in the future?"

Linda responded, "I suppose I could be sure I had more than one pencil, so I would not have to borrow."

Mrs. Martinez said, "That sounds like an excellent idea."

Mrs. Martinez's goal was to get Linda to behave in ways that would not invite her teacher's anger and disapproval. Her first approach was causing a wide gap between herself and Linda, rather than inspiring Linda to improve her behavior. When Mrs. Martinez changed her attitude and approach, she was able to win Linda over to a position where she was willing to cooperate in solving a problem that would be to her benefit in the future. When her mother was able to see things from Linda's point of view, she no longer felt the need to be defensive.

Mrs. Jones learned that her nine-year-old son Jeff had been stealing. She found a quiet time when no one else was around and asked Jeff to come sit on her lap. She then told Jeff she had heard about him stealing some gum from the store. She went on to share a time when she was in the fifth grade and had stolen an eraser from a store. She added she knew she shouldn't have done it, and it made her feel very guilty, so she decided it wasn't worth it. Jeff agreed he felt the same way. Mrs. Jones then led Jeff in a discussion exploring how much gum and other merchandise the store owner had to sell in order to pay his rent and earn enough money to live on. Jeff admitted he had never thought of that. They also discussed how they wouldn't like to have others take their things. Jeff confided he did not want to steal things anymore.

Mrs. Jones was able to win Jeff over by not accusing, blaming, or lecturing. Jeff did not have to feel he was a bad person for what he had done, but was willing to explore social-interest reasons for not doing it again.

MUTUAL RESPECT

Mutual respect incorporates attitudes of (a) faith in the abilities of yourself and others; (b) interest in the point of view of others as well as your own; and (c) willingness to take responsibility and ownership for your own contribution to the problem. The best way to teach these attitudes to children is by modeling them. You will see how the concepts of timing and winning cooperation can be merged with the concept of mutual respect.

Jason, a student in Mr. Bradshaw's fifth-grade class, often lost his temper and would loudly express his hostility to others, including Mr. Bradshaw, during class. Mr. Bradshaw had tried several forms of punishment, which only seemed to intensify Jason's outbursts. He had tried sending him to the principal's office. He had tried having Jason stay after school to write five hundred sentences about controlling his temper. He finally tried demanding that Jason leave the room to sit outside the classroom on a bench until he cooled down. Jason would slam the door on his way out. When he came back into the room, his demeanor was one of belligerence, and he would soon have another angry outburst.

Mr. Bradshaw decided to try encouragement, keeping in mind the concepts of timing, winning cooperation, and mutual respect. He began by asking Jason to stay after class, when they could be alone. He owned his part of the problem by sharing with Jason how much it upset him when the outbursts disrupted the class. He asked Jason if he would be willing to work on a solution with him. Jason was not yet willing to cooperate and showed his hostility by claiming he couldn't help it that the kids made him so mad. Mr. Bradshaw agreed he could understand that feeling, because sometimes other people made him very angry also. Jason glanced up at Mr. Bradshaw with surprise and relief showing in his eyes. Mr. Bradshaw went on to share with Jason that he was aware of certain things happening in his body when he got angry, such as a knot in his stomach and stiffening in his shoulders. He asked Jason if he was aware of things happening to his body when he got angry. Jason couldn't think of any. He then asked Jason if he would be willing to try an experiment and pay attention to what happened to his body the next time he lost his temper. Jason said he would. They agreed to get together after school the next time it happened so that Jason could share what he discovered.

It was five days before Jason had another angry outburst in class. This was a long time for Jason to go without an outburst. He had felt belonging and significance just because Mr. Bradshaw had taken the time to work with him in a friendly, respectful manner. He didn't feel the need to find belonging through misbehavior for a while.

After his next outburst Jason told Mr. Bradshaw he had noticed that he started clenching his fists and his teeth when he was getting angry. Mr. Bradshaw asked Jason if he would be willing to catch himself next time he started to get angry, and to take responsibility for himself by stepping outside the door until he had cooled off. Mr. Bradshaw added that he wouldn't have to ask permission, because he would know what Jason was doing and had faith in him to handle it all by himself.

The next day Jason stepped outside the door three times, remaining outside for three to five minutes before coming back into the classroom, noticeably calm. He continued taking this responsibility and would leave the classroom four or five times a week. It was three weeks before he lost his temper and shouted out at a classmate, forgetting to step outside.

Mr. Bradshaw talked with Jason during lunch recess and commented on how well he had been doing. He added that everyone makes mistakes while learning and asked if he would be willing to keep working for improvement. Jason agreed. Mr. Bradshaw reported that for the rest of the year Jason would occasionally step outside the door, but had very few outbursts. When Jason would come back in the room after cooling off, Mr. Bradshaw would wink at him and smile. Jason did not become perfect, but improved significantly. Mr. Bradshaw was especially pleased because rapport between them improved so that their total relationship became more enjoyable.

IMPROVEMENT, NOT PERFECTION

The above example also illustrates the concept of working for improvement, instead of expecting perfection. Perfection is such an unrealistic expectation, and very discouraging to those who feel they must live up to it. Children would rather not try at all than experience constant discouragement because they don't live up to an adult's expectation of perfection.

Recognition of improvement is encouraging and inspires children to continue their efforts.

Mrs. Bradley was feeling very discouraged because her son, Bill, was getting into trouble at school. His teacher was punishing him by having him write fifty sentences every time he misbehaved by talking or being disruptive. Bill's response was similar to Mark's (referred to in the last chapter). He also felt rebellious and would refuse to do the sentences—so his teacher would double the number. Mrs. Bradley was worried that he was becoming a delinquent, so she started scolding him. Bill was now getting punished at home and at school. He rebelled further by acting like he didn't care, and he hated school.

Mrs. Bradley finally asked for a parent-teacher conference. During the conference she asked the teacher what percentage of Bill's behavior was "bad." The teacher said, "About fifteen percent."

Mrs. Bradley was amazed to realize the negative reputation Bill was getting (and living up to) because more attention was being paid to the 15 percent misbehavior than to the 85 percent good behavior.

Mrs. Bradley was also involved in a parent study group. Unlike Mark's teacher, Bill's teacher was very much interested in hearing about logical consequences. They agreed to develop a positive plan for working with Bill. During another conference, with Bill present, they all agreed that every time he was disruptive or disrespectful in class, he would make up for it by doing something to contribute, such as doing tasks for the teacher, tutoring another member of the class who needed help, or teaching a segment of a lesson.

Bill's misbehavior was *redirected* into contributing behavior. He had very few behavior problems after that. This teacher also started having class meetings, so problems that did occur were solved by the class as a whole.

We can see from this example how negative punishment encourages rebellion and is very discouraging to the child, the parent, and the teacher. It also illustrates several concepts that are effective in encouraging children to feel belonging and to develop responsible behavior. The concepts used, which have already been explained, are mutual respect, problem solving, encouragement, and logical consequences. Other positive concepts that were used in this example will now be explained.

WHAT YOU SEE IS WHAT YOU GET

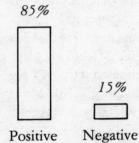

When you spend 85 percent of your time and energy focusing on the 15 percent that is negative, the negative will grow and the positive will soon disappear. *What you see is what you get.* On the other hand, if you focus 85 percent of your time and energy on the positive, it won't be long before the negative disappears and the positive will grow to 100 percent because that is all you see. *It is very encouraging to yourself and others when you focus on the positive.*

REDIRECTING MISBEHAVIOR

Look for the strengths in every child's behavior. Children who are disruptive often have good leadership skills. When you see that, it is not too difficult to work with a child and help him redirect his behavior in a contributing direction. A peer counseling program (which is described in the appendix) was based on this concept. Teachers recommended their students who had leadership skills but were using them in a disruptive direction. These students were trained to be peer counselors and used their leadership skills to help other students.

One preschool teacher mastered this concept and used it many times. Debbie didn't want to clean up her messes after art activities. The teacher put Debbie in charge and taught her how to teach the other children exactly what to do. Sean was always knocking other peoples' blocks over. The teacher made Sean the block patrol leader. His job was to teach other children how to cooperate when they played with the blocks and when it was time to pick them up.

MAKING UP FOR IT

This is very close to redirecting misbehavior, but gets the child more involved in the problem-solving process. When children do something irresponsible or disrespectful, give them the opportunity to make up for it by doing something that will make the person they offended feel better. When Bill was disruptive in class, he made the teacher's job more difficult. He was given the opportunity to make up for it by doing something to make the teacher's job easier. This does not work if the adult's attitude is punitive. It is very effective when the adult's attitude is friendly and respectful and when the child is involved in the decision.

Judy and Linda threw oranges at a neighbor's car. During a problem-solving discussion, they decided they would make up for it by washing the car.

Five boys in an elementary school were caught defacing classroom doors. The janitor let them make up for it by helping him paint the doors. The janitor's attitude was so respectful that he inspired these boys to take pride in their work and to discourage other children from vandalizing.

SOCIAL PRESSURE

It is especially difficult to use the most effective procedures with children when under social pressure. When friends, neighbors, relatives, or other teachers are observing our interaction with misbehaving children, we feel our effectiveness as a mother or teacher will be judged on how well we handle the situation. It is easy, under these circumstances, to feel that these observers expect immediate perfection—so the pressure is on. We may use punishment to satisfy the observers, since it appears to achieve the quickest results.

It takes a great deal of courage to think clearly during a time of social pressure and to do what will achieve the most effective results.

Last summer we went backpacking with several friends. Our ten-year-old son, Mark, was a very good sport and carried his pack the long six miles into the canyon. When we were getting ready for the long, steep trek back out, Mark complained about how uncomfortable his pack was. His dad jokingly remarked, "You can take it. You're the son of a Marine." Mark was in too much pain to think this was very funny, but he started the climb anyway. He hadn't gone very far ahead of us when we heard his pack come crashing down the hill toward us. I thought he had fallen and asked what had happened. Mark angrily cried, "Nothing! It hurts!" He continued climbing without his pack. Everyone else observed this with interest. One adult offered to carry the pack for him. I was feeling very embarrassed—and under the additional social pressure of having written a book on Positive Discipline!

I remembered that the most important thing was to solve the problem in a way that would help Mark feel encouraged and responsible.

I first asked the rest of the party to please hike on ahead so that we could handle the problem in private. We then used the Four Steps for Winning Cooperation.

I said to Mark, "I'll bet you feel really angry that we wouldn't pay serious attention when you tried to tell us your pack hurt before we even started."

Mark agreed.

I told him I didn't blame him and would feel exactly the same way under the circumstances.

His dad said he was sorry and asked for another chance to solve the problem. They figured out a way to stuff his coat over the sore part to cushion the pack. Mark carried the pack the rest of the way with very few, minor complaints.

When under social pressure, get away from the audience. Leave the scene yourself or respectfully request that others leave so that you can solve the problem privately.

SPECIAL TIME FOR MUTUAL SHARING

The two parts of this concept are:

1. Making a child feel special by being singled out for sharing
2. Sharing yourself as well as showing interest in the child

One of the most encouraging things parents can do for their children is to spend regular, special time with them. This could be fifteen to thirty minutes after school each day or twice a week. Or it could be one to several hours regularly scheduled every weekend. The particular time and amount would be individual for each family. The important part is that children know exactly when they can count on time that has been set aside especially for them.

This technique seems so simple and yet can be so

effective. Many teachers have reported that simply spending a few minutes after school with a child for mutual sharing has helped the child feel encouraged enough to stop misbehaving, even though the misbehavior is not mentioned during this time.

Mrs. Petersen was concerned about a child in her room whose mistaken goal was power. Debbie often refused to do her work and openly displayed hostility with sneers and sullen looks. Mrs. Petersen asked Debbie to stay after school one day. Debbie stayed, looking as if she were ready for a battle. Mrs. Petersen did not mention any problem behavior; she instead asked Debbie if she would tell her about the most fun thing she had done the night before. Debbie would not answer. Mrs. Petersen said, "Well, I would like to tell you what I did for fun last night." She then went on to share something she had done with her family the night before. Debbie still refused to respond. Mrs. Petersen told Debbie she could leave, but she would like to talk to her again for a few minutes the next day after school.

Mrs. Petersen felt discouraged, thinking the exchange had not been very helpful. However, the next day she noticed Debbie no longer had a chip on her shoulder and did not display any hostility. After school Debbie showed Mrs. Petersen a picture she had drawn of herself and a friend riding bikes. She explained this was the most fun thing she had done the night before. Mrs. Petersen then shared another fun thing she had done.

If you analyze it, you will understand why such a brief exchange can have such dramatic results. First, the child feels singled out for special attention. The child may reject this special attention at first because of his or her suspicion that it will probably be another session for blaming and lecturing. Second, the child experiences the *unexpected* when the teacher ignores behavior problems. Third, adults often show interest in having children share, but they don't demonstrate mutual respect by being self-disclosing. It is very encouraging to have someone share part of himself or herself with you. This short exchange helps a child feel belonging and significance.

It is suggested that teachers spend a few minutes of mutual-sharing time with each student in their class during the year. Start with the children who seem the most discouraged, but keep track to make sure you don't miss anyone.

Parents can apply the concept of mutual-sharing time as a bedtime routine.

When Mrs. Bruner tucks her children into bed at night, she asks them first to share the saddest thing that happened to them during the day and then the happiest thing. She then shares her saddest and happiest events.

At first her children went overboard on this opportunity to complain about sad things and would sometimes end up crying. She would patiently wait for them to calm down and then suggest, "Tomorrow night, when you don't feel so upset, we'll talk about it some more to see if we can figure out some solutions. Now tell me your happiest thing." If the child couldn't think of a happy thing, Mrs. Bruner would share her happy event. After the children got used to this routine, the sad events were reported in a matter-of-fact way, followed by working on ideas for solving or avoiding a similar problem in the future. The children soon enjoyed sharing their happy events more than their sad events.

ENCOURAGEMENT VERSUS PRAISE

For many years there has been a great campaign for the virtues of praise in helping children gain a positive self-concept and improve their behavior. This is another time when we must "beware of what works." Praise may inspire some children to improve their behavior.

The problem is that they become pleasers and approval "junkies." These children (and later these adults) develop self-concepts that are totally dependent on the opinions of others. Other children resent and rebel against praise, either because they don't want to live up to the expectations of others or because they fear they can't compete with those who seem to get praise so easily.

Even though praise may seem to "work," we must consider the long-range effects.

The alternative that considers long-range effects is encouragement. The long-range effect of encouragement is self-confidence. The long-range effect of praise is dependence on others.

The successful use of encouragement requires adult attitudes of respect, interest in the child's point of view, and a desire to influence skills that will lead the child to self-confident independence.

Some characteristics of both praise and encouragement are outlined below in order to offer guidelines for evaluating the examples that follow.

Encouragement	Praise
Self-evaluation ("Tell me about it.") ("What do you think?")	**Evaluation by others** ("I like it.")

Encouragement	*Praise*
Addresses Deed Appreciation— Respectful ("Thank you for helping.") ("Good job.") ("Who can show me the proper way to sit?")	**Addresses Doer Expectation— Patronizing** ("You are such a good boy.") ("Good girl.") ("I like the way Suzie is sitting.")
Empathy ("What do you think and feel?") ("I can see you enjoyed that.")	**Conformity** ("You did it right.") ("I'm so proud of you.")
Self-disclosing "I" messages ("I appreciate your help.")	**Judgmental "I" messages** ("I like the way you are sitting.")
Asks Questions ("Who can show me how we should be sitting when we are ready?")	**"Should" Statements** ("You should be sitting quietly.")

The differences between encouragement and praise can be difficult to grasp for those who believe in praise and have seen the positive effects. Even those who want to change from praise to encouragement find it awkward to stop and think before making statements that have become habitual.

It may help to keep the following questions in mind when wondering whether the statements you make to children are praise or encouragement:

· Am I inspiring self-evaluation or dependence on the evaluation of others?
· Am I being respectful or patronizing?
· Am I seeing the child's point of view or only my own?
· Would I make this comment to a friend?

I have found the last question especially helpful. The comments we make to friends usually fit the criteria for encouragement.

ENCOURAGEMENT VERSUS CRITICISM

It is a mistake to think the best way to help children do better is to criticize what they do wrong. Many argue that constructive criticism is helpful. Sid Simon has an excellent definition for constructive criticism—constrictive crudicism.

Dr. John Lewis Lund, in his book, *Avoiding Emotional Divorce,* explains that constructive criticism is a contradiction in terms. Constructive means to build up. Criticism means to tear down. He also points out that criticism is a cancer and that it does not change behavior. I strongly recommend his book, not only for his excellent chapter on criticism but for many other excellent ideas on understanding and improving relationships.

This does not mean we shouldn't let children know when there is room for improvement. It does mean we don't have to make them feel worse in order to get them to do better.

As parents and teachers we are required to go beyond encouragement. We are responsible for helping children learn and improve academic and social skills. However, encouragement is usually the best way to inspire a child to want to do better. If other methods are used, such as those that follow, they will be most effective if the child has first been won over through encouragement so that he or she will be receptive.

METHODS FOR HELPING CHILDREN LEARN AND IMPROVE

1. Take Time for Training

This is not as obvious as it may sound. Adults often expect children to accomplish tasks for which there has not been adequate training. This is more typical in homes than in schools. Parents may expect children to clean their rooms, but never teach them how. They may expect good manners when the only teaching has been nagging.

Dr. Stephen Glenn points out in his lectures that parents often tell children what expectations they have without ever bothering to specify exactly how these expectations should be met. There is often a great communication gap. When Dad tells his daughter to clean up the garage, they may have very different ideas of what this means. Taking time for specific training can eliminate the misunderstanding.

Dr. Glenn further demonstrated the communication gap by the following conversation:

Mom: Bill, clean up your room!

Bill: I did. (Meaning: I can walk through it.)

Mom: No you didn't. (Meaning: I can't eat off the floor.)

Taking time for training means being very specific about your terms and expectations. One mother spends several years helping her children make their beds. She gives them pointers such as, "What would happen if you pulled here?" (It would straighten a wrinkle.) She buys bedspreads with plaids or stripes so that her children can learn to have straight lines along the edges. By the time they are six, they have had enough training to know how to make their beds almost well enough to pass an army inspection.

When you ask children to clean the kitchen, make sure they know what that means to you. To them it may mean simply putting the dishes in the sink. Many parents get upset when their children do a terrible job with chores, even though they have never taken time for training.

Taking time for training also includes telling your children when you are going to change your methods. Mrs. Roberts heard me talk about how important it is to allow children to dress themselves. Her daughter, Connie, was in the third grade. Mrs. Roberts wasn't still dressing Connie, but she was laying her clothes out for her every night. She decided she wouldn't do this anymore, but didn't tell Connie. The next morning she heard Connie yell in an irritated voice, "Mother, where are my clothes?"

Mrs. Roberts replied very respectfully, "They are in the closet, dear. I'm sure you can find them yourself."

Connie retorted, "Mother, when you decide to do these things, will you please let me know?"

Connie was right. It is a good idea to respectfully discuss changes with whomever is involved before implementing them.

2. Ask for Self-Evaluation

If you feel there has been adequate training, check it out by asking the child, "What is your understanding of what needs to be done?"

Cory brought her writing assignment on the letter *g* to her third-grade teacher, Mrs. Tuttle, who looked at the paper and asked Cory to point out her favorite one. After Cory pointed to her favorite *g,* Mrs. Tuttle said, "May I point out my favorite one?" Cory happily agreed. Mrs. Tuttle pointed to another nicely executed *g.* Next Mrs. Tuttle pointed to a *g* with a double tail and asked Cory to tell her about that one.

Cory showed her surprise by covering her mouth with her hand as she said, "Oh." Mrs. Tuttle asked Cory if she could fix it by herself, or did she need help? Cory said she could and went back to her desk to fix it.

Mrs. Tuttle did not point out only the error. She focused on strengths first and then asked Cory to evaluate the error herself.

If we ask children what areas they need to work on for improvement, they can usually tell us without being told.

3. Build on Strengths, not Weaknesses

The foregoing example incorporates this concept. When you point out what has been done well, children usually want to continue doing as well or better.

4. Ask Questions

You will achieve greater participation and understanding if you ask questions of children rather than making statements. When children answer your questions, they are actively involved. When you make statements, they are passively involved. When they answer questions, you have an opportunity to hear whether or not their understanding is the same as yours. For example, instead of telling your child to clean up the kitchen, ask, "What do you think needs to be done before the kitchen is clean?"

Your child may say, "Wash the dishes."

You can then ask, "What about the things on the table?"

Your child will admit, "Oh, well, I guess they need to be put away."

You can reply, "Right, and what about the things on the stove? And what do you need to do about the table, cabinets, and stove surfaces after everything is put away?"

By using this technique, you are also taking time for training. In the next two chapters you will see how important it is to get children actively involved by asking questions in class and family meetings.

5. The Courage to Be Imperfect

We are all imperfect. What we need to achieve is the courage to accept imperfection. This is one of the most encouraging concepts, and yet one of the hardest to achieve in our society. There isn't a perfect human being in the world, yet everyone is demanding it of themselves and others. We set ourselves up for disappointment and frustrations because of this impossible ideal of perfection. Improvement, yes. Perfection, no.

In our society we are taught to be ashamed of mistakes. We should instead learn and teach children to be excited about mistakes as opportunities to learn. Wouldn't it be wonderful to hear an adult say to a child, "You made a mistake. That is fantastic. What can we learn from it?" And I do mean *we*. We are partners in most of the mistakes made by children. Many mistakes are made because we haven't taken time for training and encouragement. We often provoke rebellion instead of inspiring improvement. Model the courage to accept imperfection so that children will learn from you that mistakes truly are an opportunity to learn. Using the three R's of Recovery (explained in chapter 9) is an excellent way to model the courage to be imperfect.

If none of the above methods is effective, it is likely the child is basing his or her behavior on one of the four mistaken goals and needs more encouragement, help from a family or class meeting, or other methods taught throughout the book.

Group Exercises

Encouragement versus Praise versus Criticism

Draw a picture of a house the way a first-grade child might, including mistakes and distortions. Ask the group to give examples of what they might say if a child came to them with this picture and said, "Mommy (or Daddy or teacher), look at my picture." Point out that you want examples of praise, encouragement, and criticism, so that no one will feel embarrassed if they can't think of an encouraging statement. After each example, have the group decide whether the statement is an example of encouragement, praise, or criticism, based on the criteria in this chapter.

A Child's Point of View

An excellent way to help adults remember a child's point of view is to remember their own childhoods. Instruct the group as follows:

Close your eyes and think back to your childhood. Remember an incident between you and an adult at home or school when you felt discouraged, misunderstood, humiliated, or treated unfairly, or any combination of the above. Relive the experience. Remember exactly what happened and how you felt. Relive those feelings. (Allow about two minutes of silence for this.)

Now with your eyes still closed, remember another incident between an adult and you as a child when you felt encouraged, understood, appreciated, special, inspired to do better, or any combination of the above. Relive this experience. Remember exactly what happened and how you felt. Relive those feelings. (Allow another two minutes of silence.)

Ask for volunteers who would be willing to share first their discouraging memories. After sharing, pick out the common aspects of the memories. How were the feelings similar? What was similar about what the adults did?

The common aspects of discouraging experiences are usually those mentioned above: The child feels misunderstood, humiliated, or treated unfairly. Another common aspect is that children usually do not feel inspired to improve as a result of these discouraging experiences, even though that is usually the adult's goal. Many have shared how they gave up trying to improve a skill such as piano, reading, penmanship, sports, and so on because of the discouraging criticism they received from an adult.

The common aspects of encouraging experiences are also those mentioned above. The child usually feels understood, appreciated, and special. These experiences often inspire children to do better and to pursue worthwhile skills or goals. Another amazing aspect is that most of the encouraging experiences involve very little time on the part of the adult to offer a few words of recognition and appreciation.

QUESTIONS FOR REVIEW OF CHAPTER 6

1. What is a misbehaving child?

2. What is the hidden message behind the misbehavior?

3. What did Dreikurs think was the most important skill adults could learn to help children?

4. Discuss the importance of timing.

5. What are the Four Steps for Winning Cooperation?

6. What are the necessary adult attitudes for the above four steps to be effective?

7. What are the necessary adult attitudes for mutual respect?

8. Why is a special time for mutual sharing so powerful for encouraging children and motivating them to improve their behavior?

9. What are the dangers of praise?

10. What are the long-range effects of encouragement?

11. Name some of the differences between praise and encouragement.

12. What are the questions you should ask as a self-check to determine whether your statements are encouragement or praise?

13. Name and describe the five methods for helping children learn and improve.

14. If the five methods are not effective, what is the likely reason?

15. Why is it important to have the courage to accept imperfection?

16. Why would it be helpful to teach children that mistakes are opportunities to learn rather than something to be ashamed of?

Chapter Seven

CLASS MEETINGS

By now you know that the effectiveness of the positive approach depends on adult attitudes of mutual respect and concern for the long-range effects on children. It has been promised that children who experience the kind of interaction outlined in this book will learn self-discipline, cooperation, responsibility, and problem-solving skills.

The culmination of all these promises and attitudes is most fully realized and experienced in regularly scheduled family and class meetings. Such meetings provide the best possible circumstances for adults and children to learn the democratic procedure of cooperation, mutual respect, responsibility, and social interest. These are the important long-range goals that inspire many parents and teachers to try class and family meetings, but there are many more immediate fringe benefits.

Teachers, for example, are relieved to get out of the roles of policeman, judge, jury, and executioner. Whenever students come with problems, teachers can simply request that the problem be put on the class meeting agenda. This alone is enough of an immediate solution to give satisfaction, while providing for a cooling-off period before trying to solve the problem.

Students are often able to solve problems much better than the teacher, simply because there are more of them. They have many excellent ideas when they are allowed and encouraged to express them. Teachers are frequently amazed at the academic and social skills children learn in class meetings. Because the children are intensively involved in solving problems that are so relevant for them, they learn listening skills, language development, extended thinking, logical consequences of behavior, memory skills, and objective thinking about the value and mechanics of learning.

Teachers find that children are much more willing to cooperate when they have been involved in the decisions, even when the final solution is one that has been suggested by the teacher many times in the past to no avail.

Before outlining things to do in order to have a successful class meeting, we will look at some attitudes and actions to avoid:

1. Do not use the class meeting as another platform for lecturing and moralizing. It is essential to be as objective and nonjudgmental as possible. This does not mean you cannot have input into the meetings. You can still put items on the agenda and give your opinion and have an equal vote.

2. Do not use the class meeting as a guise to continue excessive control. Children see through this approach and will not cooperate.

Class meetings should be held every day (or at least three times a week). If class meetings are not held often enough, students will be discouraged from putting items on the agenda, because it will take too long to get to them. A cooling-off period of at least three days is recommended before discussing a problem. It is discouraging to have to wait much longer than three days. (A shorter cooling-off period is recommended for younger children. In kindergarten, one hour is often long enough.)

Decisions are made by a majority vote. This does not cause feelings of division in a class meeting when a positive atmosphere has been created. It provides a great opportunity for students to learn that everyone doesn't think and feel the same way they do. Students also learn that it is impossible to have everyone agree, but they can still cooperate.

Several ideas must be explained and discussed with children before actual agenda items are dealt with. During the first meeting, get the children involved as much as possible while teaching them the purposes of class meetings, the importance of mutual respect, how to give compliments, how to solve problems with logical consequences, the Three Rs of Logical Consequences, how to use the agenda, and the importance of a cooling-off period.

> **Purposes of Class Meetings:**
>
> 1. To give compliments
> 2. To help each other
> 3. To solve problems
> 4. To plan events

Many teachers start every meeting by asking the children, "What are the two main purposes of class meetings." The two main purposes are to help each other and to solve problems.

SOME OF THE GOALS OF CLASS MEETINGS

Teaching Mutual Respect

Teach children the meaning of mutual respect by having a discussion of the following questions:

1. Why is it disrespectful when more than one person talks at the same time? (We can't hear what everyone is saying. The person who is supposed to be talking feels others don't care, and so on.)

2. Why is it disrespectful to disturb others? (They can't concentrate and learn from what is going on.)

3. Why is it important to raise your hand before speaking in a large group? (To achieve order and remember whose turn it is.)

4. Why is it important to listen when others are speak-

ing? (So that we can learn from each other, to show respect for each other, and because we like to have others listen to us.)

Giving Compliments

Spend some time with children exploring the meaning of compliments. This can be done informally during the first meeting. Compliments should consist of acknowledgment of others in the following areas:

- Accomplishments
- Helpfulness
- Sharing

Have the children brainstorm for specific examples in each of these areas. Then teach them to use the words, "I would like to compliment *(a person's name)* for *(something specific that person did)."* Using these words helps children stay on the task of recognizing what others do, rather than what they wear. I have visited hundreds of classrooms to observe class meetings in schools that have adopted this program. In every classroom where they did not use the prescribed phrasing, the compliments were less specific and more superficial.

At first many children might say, "I would like to compliment Jill for being my friend." Let this go for a while during the learning process, but eventually the group could again brainstorm on how to be specific about what a friend *does* that we would like to recognize and appreciate.

The teacher may start by giving several compliments (from notes taken during the day, when noticing things children did that would merit recognition). Many teachers model giving compliments every day, making sure they eventually cover every child in their classroom, a few each day.

During the first meeting, have everyone give at least one compliment to make sure they know how to do it. If anyone has difficulty, have the class help by asking if anyone has any ideas on something that happened to this child during the day that he could compliment someone for, like playing with him during recess. After this, compliments can be optional.

It is also a good idea to teach children to say thank you after receiving a compliment. You may have several class meetings just for compliments while the children learn this process.

Many teachers have shared that compliments alone have been significant in creating a more positive atmosphere in their classrooms. After the initial awkwardness, children love looking for, giving, and receiving positive recognition. *Where else do they get this valuable training?*

Teaching Logical Consequences

Teach the children to use logical consequences before trying to solve any problems. Start by having them brainstorm regarding natural consequences by asking what happens in the following circumstances if no one interferes:

- If you stand in the rain? (You get wet.)
- If you play on the freeway? (You might get killed.)
- If you don't sleep? (You get tired.)
- If you don't eat? (You get hungry.)

Next explain that logical consequences are things that can be done to help others learn to be responsible for their behavior, when it is not appropriate to let them experience a natural consequence. Explain the Three Rs of Logical Consequences, as explained in chapter 6. It is a good idea to make a poster of the Three Rs for the children to refer to. Then have them brainstorm and discuss logical consequences for the following problems:

· Someone who writes on a desk
· Someone who rides the tether ball
· Someone who doesn't do their work during class time
· Someone who is late for school

It is much easier to give the children practice by working on hypothetical situations, so that there is a lack of emotional involvement and blame. After receiving as many suggestions as possible, go over each one and have the children see how well they fit the criteria for the Three Rs for Logical Consequences. Have them discuss their reasons why they think each suggestion is or isn't *related, respectful,* and *reasonable.* Also have them discuss how each suggestion will be helpful to the person, or will it be hurtful? Have the class decide which suggestions should be eliminated because they do not meet the guidelines of the Three Rs or because they are in some other way hurtful.

THE HOW-TOS OF CLASS MEETINGS

Using The Agenda

Introduce the agenda to the group. Some teachers reserve space on the blackboard. Others keep a sheet of paper on a clipboard where it is easily accessible.

Explain to the children that you are going to teach them to solve problems rather than trying to solve all of them by yourself. From now on, instead of coming to you with problems, they can put their name on the agenda, followed by a few words to help them remember what the problem is about. Warn them that at first they may forget and still come to you for solutions, but you will remind them to put it on the agenda. Eventually they will get tired of hearing you sound like a broken record and will remember to put problems on the agenda. These problems will then be solved during the class meetings.

Anytime teachers or parents ask me for solutions to problems they are having with children, my pat answer is, "Put it on the agenda." Children will come up with the best solutions and are then willing to cooperate because they were involved in the decision. When solutions do not seem to work, simply put the problem back on the agenda for more discussion and problem solving in a cooperative atmosphere. When you yourself put items on the agenda, be sure to *own* the problem, rather than trying to place blame. Children feel good about helping you with *your* problem. The items on the agenda are to be covered in chronological order in the amount of time allotted. Any problem that is not finished before the end of the meeting will be continued the next day.

Quite often, by the time an agenda item comes up for

discussion, the person who put it on the agenda will say that it has already been taken care of. Some adults say, "Fine," and go on to the next item. Others ask the child if she would like to share the solution.

Using the Cooling-Off Period

Explain why problems can't be solved when people are upset. With older children you can ask them why. With younger children, explain that the purpose of waiting a few hours or a few days before solving problems on the agenda is to give people a chance to cool off and calm down so that problems can be solved respectfully.

Meeting in a Circle

It is important that students sit in a circle for class meetings. Remaining at their desks not only creates physical barriers, which retard the process, but I have yet to see a class meeting where students could keep from fidgeting with items in or on their desk while remaining at their desks.

Take time to train students to move their desks with as little noise and confusion as possible. Some classes spend several days practicing. I have seen every kind of desk moved from all kinds of arrangements so that students could sit in a circle facing each other. The shortest time was fifteen seconds. Most can do it in thirty to forty-five seconds.

Training can involve several steps. First you might ask the students what they think they need to do to move with as little noise and confusion as possible. They will usually come up with all the things necessary for a smooth transition. Then ask them how many times they think they will need to practice before they can implement their good ideas.

Some teachers like to assign seats. On the first day they have one student at a time move his or her desk and put the chair into the assigned space. Other teachers have a few move at a time, by row or by team. If they are noisy and disruptive, have them practice until they solve the problems. Once they have learned to do it quietly, they can all move at once.

Class-Meeting Structure

The steps listed below were developed by Frank Meder and are helpful guidelines teachers can use for successful class meetings. Before I learned these steps, many of the class meetings I conducted failed because there was not enough structure. When students were not immediately impressed with what I was trying to accomplish and would become disruptive, I would give up, commenting to the students, "Well, obviously you don't want a class meeting now. We'll try again later when *you* are ready." In other words, not only did I not take responsibility for my own lack of readiness, but I also gave in to anarchy.

1. Begin with compliments. Students who want to give someone a compliment will raise their hand and the teacher or student leader should go around the circle and call on everyone who has a hand raised. Go around the circle once and call on everyone who has a hand raised. When going around the circle it is important to start and stop at the same place. This avoids the accusations of

"unfair" when a teacher calls on students at random and arbitrarily chooses when to stop. There is always one who claims he didn't get called on. Some teachers have their students pass a pencil or a beanbag, instead of raising their hands. The person who has the object in his hands may either speak or pass it on.

2. Read the first item on the agenda. Ask the person who wrote the item if it is still a problem. If she says no, go on to the next item. If another person is involved, ask her to explain her side of the story.

3. Ask the person who has been "accused" if she has a suggestion for a solution. If she does, ask the group to vote on her suggestion. If the majority vote agrees with the suggestion, go on to the next item.

4. If a solution is not suggested or if the majority vote does not go along with the suggestion, go around the circle twice for comments and suggestions. Start with the person who wrote the item on the agenda and end just before this person after going around the circle twice.

5. Write down every suggestion exactly as it is given. You will find suggestions on what to do if children are being hurtful rather than helpful (by not suggesting true logical consequences) under "Common Questions" at the end of this chapter.

6. Read all the suggestions before asking for a vote. Instruct children to vote for only one suggestion. Read the suggestions again one at a time and write down the number of people voting for each suggestion.

7. When the final vote is in, ask the person for whom the solution was suggested when he would like to do it and give two possibilities to choose from, such as today or tomorrow, or during recess or after school. There is some psychological benefit in giving students a choice of

when they would like to complete the consequence. It gives them a sense of positive power and commitment.

Frank's method provides a process that can be followed step by step. However, it is not so rigid as to eliminate room for teacher individuality and creativity. Teachers all over California have learned this process and then taught me new ideas as I observed them in action. Many of their ideas are shared in this and other chapters.

Some teachers do not feel comfortable with a majority vote. After all the suggestions are in, they ask the "accused" child which suggestion he or she thinks would be the most helpful. These teachers claim that the child usually chooses the most logical, even when it is not necessarily the easiest. Other teachers say this does not work for them, because their children choose the easiest and it does not seem to help change the behavior.

Hand signals are a great way for all the children to let their opinions be known during a class meeting without being disrespectful or disruptive. Teach the children to move their hands crossing back and forth over their lap when they want to express disagreement. When they agree with what is being said they can move their fist up and down above their shoulder.

Hand signals are offensive to some teachers. They claim they couldn't stand to have someone waving their hands and arms around while they were talking. I can understand their concern. It would certainly bother me, especially if the movement was indicating disagreement with what I was saying. However, if you closely observe children engaged in this process, you will discover that it does not seem distracting to them.

After observing a class meeting where a child was

asked to apologize in front of the class for a misbehavior that was put on the agenda, one adult objected. She felt it was humiliating for the child. I invited her to ask the child and other members of the class if it bothered them to apologize in front of everyone. The class unanimously agreed that it did not bother them. The point is that we should finely tune our awareness of *the child's world,* rather than projecting our own world onto them.

TEACHER SKILLS

We have discussed many of the skills students need to learn for successful class meetings. There are several teacher skills that greatly enhance class meetings. It is most important to model what you are hoping the children will learn—mutual respect and cooperation. Teachers should model **courtesy statements,** such as *please, thank you, you are welcome,* and so on.

One of the most important skills that both models mutual respect and allows children to develop their capabilities is **open-ended questioning.** Any statement you might like to make can be put in the form of a question. If you want to let children know you think they are being too noisy, ask, "How many think it is getting too noisy in here?" It is especially effective if you ask the question both ways. If you ask how many think it is okay, also ask how many think it is not okay. The less you let your own biases show, the more you allow children to think. It is amazing how often children come up with the same kind of lecturing and moralizing statements they reject when they are spoken by an adult.

Open-ended questions can change an atmosphere

from negative to positive, as in the following example. A teacher requested help with a student who was causing a great deal of trouble on the playground. Dr. John Platt felt the best way to handle the problem was through a class meeting. This teacher had never held a class meeting, so Dr. Platt used this opportunity to demonstrate.

He asked Billy to leave the classroom. The general rule is that you do not discuss a child who is not here, but in this case he knew that a positive atmosphere had not been created and did not want to take chances that Billy would be hurt by the comments. The class meeting was started by asking who was the biggest troublemaker in the class. They all chorused, "Billy." They were then asked what kind of things Billy did to cause trouble. They mentioned fighting, stealing balls, swearing, calling names, and so on. These first questions allow the children to express what they have been thinking and feeling.

The next questions allowed the children an opportunity to think and feel in a positive direction. "Why do you think Billy does these things?"

The answers included such things as, "Because he is mean." "He is a bully." Finally one student said, "Maybe it is because he doesn't have any friends." Another student chimed in that Billy was a foster child.

When the children were asked to discuss what it meant to be a foster child, they offered such ideas as how hard it must be to leave your family, move so much, and so forth. They were now expressing understanding for Billy, instead of hostility.

Everyone in the class raised his hand when asked, "How many of you would be willing to help Billy?" A list was made on the board of all their suggestions of what they could do to help. These included walking to and from school with Billy, playing with him during recess, and eating lunch with him. Specific volunteers were then listed after each suggestion.

Later, Billy was told the class had discussed the problems he had been having on the playground. When he was asked if he had any idea how many of the students wanted to help him, he looked at the ground and replied, "Probably none of them." When he was told that every one of the students wanted to help him, he looked up with wide eyes and asked as though he couldn't believe it, "Every one?"

When the whole class decided to help Billy by being his friend, he felt such a sense of belonging that his behavior improved dramatically.

Another skill is to be willing to **take ownership** for some problems you have been trying to lay on the children. A seventh-grade teacher shared her experience with toothpick chewing. It drove her crazy, because not only did she think it looked disgusting, but she found toothpicks lying all over the classroom and school grounds. It was a problem for her, but not for her students. She had lectured and implored the students many times to please stop chewing toothpicks. Nothing happened. Finally she put it on the agenda and admitted she could understand it was not a problem for them, but she would appreciate it if they would help her with a solution to her problem. Because they had only fifty minutes for class, they could not spend more than ten minutes a day for class meeting; so quite often they didn't come up with a final solution for several days. On the third day of discussing toothpicks, one of the students asked the teacher if she had seen anyone chewing toothpicks lately. She realized and admitted that she hadn't. This student observed that maybe the problem had been solved.

This is an excellent example of how many times just discussing a problem is enough to make everyone aware of it and to continue working toward solutions outside the class meeting setting.

Be as **nonjudgmental** as possible. When students feel they can discuss anything without being judged, they will bring many things out in the open for discussion and learning. One teacher expressed concern that if you talked about some things, such as spitting in the bathroom, it might give other students ideas they hadn't thought of before. As we talked, he realized that the students knew what was going on and that not talking about it openly would not make it go away.

Do not censor agenda items. Some adults want to censor items on the agenda that they consider "tattletale" items. What may seem like a tattletale item to you is a real concern to the child. Other adults want to eliminate items if a similar problem has been discussed before. Again, it may be similar to you, but unique to the child. The important thing to remember is that **the process is even more important than the solutions.** Even if the item seems the same to you, the children may solve it differently or more quickly because of their past experience with the process.

Finally, it is important to be able to **find the positive intent** behind every behavior. This enables children to feel validated and loved, an essential prerequisite to changing behavior. During one class meeting, the students were discussing a problem of cheating. The girl whose problem it was explained that she had looked at the words before her spelling test because she wanted to pass the test. Mr. Meder asked, "How many think it is really great that people want to pass their tests?" Most of the class raised their hands. Another boy admitted that he had been caught cheating and had had to take a test over again. Mr. Meder asked, "Did it help you out?" The boy said yes. These are two examples of finding the positive in what could be seen only as negative.

COMMON QUESTIONS

Question: Don't children need immediate solutions to their problems? I don't think my students could wait three days for their problems to come up on the agenda.

Answer: I worked with another teacher who felt the same way. She had been having class meetings right after lunch to handle all problems that occurred during lunch recess. I encouraged her to try having her students put their problems on an agenda and wait at least three days to solve them in a class meeting. She later reported that she was surprised at how much satisfaction the students demonstrated just from the simple act of writing their problem on the agenda. That was their *immediate* solution. Their body language indicated relief as they walked away from the agenda. She also reported that three days later the discussion of the problems was much more rational and helpful because tempers had cooled considerably.

Question: What if a consequence that has been decided on doesn't work effectively?

Answer: The decision should stay in effect until someone puts it back on the agenda. In one class they were having the problem of students leaning back in their chairs. The class decided that anyone who leaned back would have to stand up behind their chair. This did not work effectively, because too many children enjoyed standing up behind their chairs and it was disruptive to the class meeting. The teacher put this problem back on the agenda. The students agreed that it was disruptive and decided that anyone who leaned back would have to leave the class meetings as a reminder, but that they could come back when they were ready to sit correctly.

Question: What if someone feels that a consequence is unfair?

Answer: They can put it on the agenda. One class decided that Julia should have to write five hundred sentences that she would not cut in line. She wrote the five hundred sentences, but then she put it on the agenda that she did not think it was a fair, *related* consequence. She pointed out that since she had to do it, others might have to, and they probably wouldn't like it either. One student asked Julia if she thought it had helped her decide not to cut in line anymore. She admitted that it probably had, but the class still agreed that writing sentences was not as *reasonable* as some other consequence might be. This was an excellent example of the kind of communication, thinking, and cooperation that can be realized in group meetings.

Question: What do you do if students suggest punishment instead of logical consequences?

Answer: Eventually, when students become familiar with the process, they will usually work it out as in the foregoing example. To help teach the process, you might try asking students to state how they think their suggestion will be helpful and if it meets all Three Rs of Logical

Consequences by being *related, respectful,* and *reasonable.*
This is especially effective if it is required for every suggestion, rather than just those that seem "suspicious."
Some teachers feel this takes too much time. They write
down each suggestion given, and then the students decide which suggestions fit all the criteria of helpfulness
and logical consequences before they vote.

Question: What if students start to "gang up" on another child?

Answer: This does happen sometimes, even after the
students have learned to be positive and helpful most of
the time. During one class-meeting demonstration being
done by Frank Meder, they were discussing the problem
of a new student who had used "bad" language on the
playground. They seemed to be ganging up on her in
hurtful ways. Frank redirected them through effective
questioning. He asked, "How many know what it feels
like to be a new kid in school?" Several students commented on their experience with this. Then Frank asked
how many of them had taken the time to be her friend
and tell her about school rules. A few raised their hands.
Frank turned to the new girl and asked her if students
used bad language at her old school. She acknowledged
that they did. Frank then asked how many would be
willing to make friends with her and tell her about our
rules. Many raised their hands. They then went back to
the regular format, but the atmosphere was now very
positive and helpful. The students decided there
wouldn't be any consequences this time, because she
didn't know about their rules.

In one eighth-grade class meeting it seemed obvious
that the student being discussed felt he was being ganged
up on. I asked the students, "How many of you would

feel you were being ganged up on if you were in Bill's position right now?" Most of them raised their hands. I then asked, "How many of you would be willing to imagine yourself in the other person's position when making comments and suggestions?" They all agreed they would and admitted it was funny they hadn't thought of that before.

The students in this classroom had already decided that everyone would put their head down and close their eyes while voting, so that no one could be influenced by the vote of others or be worried that someone would get mad at them for their vote.

Question: What if a problem involves a student from another classroom?

Answer: Many schools have class meetings at the same time so other students can be invited from one classroom to the next. Before inviting another student into your classroom, have the students discuss what it might feel like to be called into another room. Have them discuss what they can do to make sure the invited student feels the purpose is to help and not to hurt.

In some classrooms, students brainstorm on positive things about the invited student so that they can start with compliments. Stuart was invited into Mrs. Petersen's classroom because some students complained that he had stomped on their sandcastle. They started by complimenting him for his achievements in sports and his leadership abilities. Mrs. Petersen then asked Stuart if he knew why he destroyed their sandcastles. He explained that one time it was an accident and another time it was because the bell had rung anyway. Stuart was asked if he had any suggestions for solving the problem. Stuart suggested he would like to be the sandcastle patrol to make sure no one destroyed sandcastles. The class agreed unanimously with his suggestion.

Starting with compliments reduces defensiveness and inspires cooperation. Some classes start all problem solving by complimenting both parties involved on the positive things others appreciate about them.

Question: How do you stop tattletales from being on the agenda?

Answer: You don't. These are so often the kind of problems that are real to students. If teachers censor agenda items, students will lose faith in the process. Also, when students use the class-meeting process, these problems lose their "tattletale" connotation because students are trying to solve them in helpful, rather than hurtful, ways.

Question: What do you do when a few students monopolize the agenda?

Answer: Put it on the agenda and let the students solve the problem. One teacher shared that she had this problem. Tommy was putting as many as ten items a day on the agenda. I told her to put it on the agenda, but she discovered that another student already had. The class decided that each person could put one thing on the agenda each day. This teacher admitted that if she had tried to solve the problem herself, she would have allowed three to five times a day, but she liked the children's solution much better.

Question: Can students put the teacher on the agenda if they have a complaint?

Answer: If teachers have captured the spirit of the class-meeting process, they will feel comfortable discussing their own mistakes as an opportunity to learn. This is excellent modeling for the students.

Frank Meder brought his students in to demonstrate a class meeting for my college class. An item on the agenda for discussion was that Frank had taken a bag of potato chips from a student during recess because of the school rule against eating on the playground. On the way back to the teacher's room he ate some of the potato chips. The consequence decided on by the class was for Mr. Meder to buy the student another bag of potato chips—but he could eat half of them first, because the bag was only half full when he got it.

Another time, a student put Mr. Meder on the agenda for making a student run around the track for misbehaving during physical education. The students decided that this was punishment rather than a logical consequence. They decided that Mr. Meder should run the track four times. Frank accepted their decision, but after running the track, he put it on the agenda and discussed that it was unfair for him to be required to run four times when the student had only had to run once. He used this as an opportunity to discuss how easy it is to get into revenge when punishment is involved.

Question: What do you do when children won't admit they did whatever they have been accused of?

Answer: Once an atmosphere of trust and helpfulness has been established, it is rare that students don't feel free to take responsibility for their actions. Before this atmosphere has been established, you might ask if anyone else in the class saw what happened. Some teachers have the students role-play what happened. The role-playing usually gets so humorous that everyone is laughing. This sometimes inspires the reluctant student to tell how it *really* happened.

You could take this opportunity to ask some questions

about why students might feel reluctant to admit they did something, such as, "How many of you would want to admit you had done something if you thought other people might want to hurt you, instead of help you?" "How many of you have had other people accuse you of doing something when you did not think you had done anything?" Many teachers have found it effective to ask the students if they would be willing to take the person's word that they didn't do it this time and put it on the agenda if it happens again.

Question: What do you do if students use the agenda as revenge? My students go to the agenda and if their name is on it, they put the person on the agenda who put them on.

Answer: This happens quite often before students learn and believe that the purpose of the agenda is to help each other, rather than to "get" each other. Many teachers solve this problem by using a shoe box for the agenda. They have students write their problem on different colored paper for different days of the week, so that they can tell which problems are the oldest. Some teachers also have students put written compliments in the box. These written compliments are read before the oral compliments are given. Most teachers who use the shoe box at first start using the open agenda as soon as they feel their students are ready for it.

Question: What should I do about students gathering at the agenda on their way into the classroom after recess?

Answer: If students are gathering at the agenda when coming into the classroom, making it difficult to start lessons, have a rule that the agenda can be used only when leaving the classroom. Sometimes just waiting until the next recess is enough of a cooling-off period for the student to decide that something wasn't serious enough to put on the agenda. Some teachers start out with this rule and then later, when the students can handle this without being disruptive, they allow them to use the agenda anytime.

Question: Is it really necessary to have class meetings every day? I'm not having that many problems and hate to take so much time.

Answer: The main reason for having class meetings every day is to teach a process. Many students do not really learn the process if there is a time span of a week between meetings. Several teachers have learned that having them every day can make the difference between success and failure. One teacher with a particularly difficult class was about to give up on class meetings until he started having them every day. He found that his students learned and trusted the process when it was done every day. The atmosphere of his class changed because the students learned positive skills, which they continued to use throughout the day.

Another teacher said she hadn't been having class meetings because she had a very cooperative class and wasn't having problems. She tried to have a class meeting when a big problem came up and found that the class could not handle it because they had not learned the process. This teacher had not understood the importance of class meetings as a process to teach children skills that enable them to solve problems when they occur.

Another teacher discovered that the reason his students weren't putting items on the agenda was that it took too long for items to come up when they had class meetings only once a week.

It is better to have class meetings every day. If there

are not any problems on the agenda, use the time after compliments for planning or discussing other issues.

Question: What if an item on the agenda involves a student who is absent?

Answer: If the absent student is the one who put the item on the agenda, cross it out and go on to the next item. If the absent student is the accused, skip it, but leave it on the agenda as the first item to be discussed when the student returns. This reduces the possibility that absences are because of the agenda. However, if you suspect that students want to be absent because their name is on the agenda, this should be discussed in a class meeting so that the class can decide what they need to do to make sure people know they want to help each other, rather than hurt each other.

Question: What if parents object?

Answer: Invite them to come and observe. Very few parents object after they have seen the class meeting in action. Some students may feel they can get special attention from their parents by complaining about being "picked on" in class meetings. Even when students try to describe class meetings accurately, it can sound like a kangaroo court to parents. Express to parents that you can understand their concern and would probably feel the same way if you hadn't had a thorough explanation. Some parents may come. Others will be reassured by your understanding and invitation.

If parents still object after visiting, or if they refuse to visit but still insist that their child cannot participate, arrange for their child to visit another classroom or the library during class meetings.

Question: What if students don't want to participate?

Answer: Students should not have a choice in this matter, just as they do not have a choice regarding their participation in math.

Question: How does this process work with kindergarten and first-grade children?

Answer: Great! I have visited many primary grades where the children were doing so well that I had to pinch myself to remember they were not really miniature sixth-graders. They were using the same vocabulary and the same problem-solving skills.

Younger children may need more help with the agenda, however. Some primary teachers have the children come to them or an aide and dictate what they would like to put on the agenda. Others have the children write their name and draw a picture to remind them of their problem. In these early grades, half the problems are often solved because the child can't remember what happened by the time their name comes up on the agenda.

Younger children may need a little more direction and guidance, so the teacher may need to be more actively involved than for older children. At the beginning of each meeting, Mrs. Binns has her first-grade students recite the purposes:

1. To help each other
2. To solve problems

They then recite the three rules:

1. Don't bring any objects to the circle
2. Only one person can speak at a time
3. All six legs must be on the floor (two human and four chair).

OTHER SUGGESTIONS

Secret Pals

Some teachers like to use the Monday class meeting for each student to draw the name of a secret pal for the week. The Friday class meeting is then used for each student to guess who her secret pal was by sharing what nice things that secret pal did for her.

Some preliminary teaching is important for this to be effective. First, have the students brainstorm on things they could do for a secret pal, such as leaving nice notes for him, sharing something with him, helping him, playing with him, smiling and saying hello every day, or leaving a piece of candy in his desk. After several ideas have been listed on the board, have each student write down at least five that they would like to do. They can tape this list onto their desk and cross off an item after they have done it. This reduces the possibility that some students will be overlooked. This has significantly increased positive feelings of friendship in many classrooms.

Chairperson

Many teachers rotate chairperson and secretarial duties. One student will be the chairperson for a week and will follow the format. The secretary is the person responsible for writing down all suggestions and final decisions.

Planning

There are certain decisions students cannot be involved in, such as curriculum (unless you want to encour-

age them to talk to the adults who make those decisions).
However, there are many areas where students could
participate in planning decisions. When students are invited to participate and help make the decisions, they are
more highly motivated to cooperate in the fulfillment of
those decisions.

I was delighted to see how one teacher carried out this
suggestion. Most classrooms have rules posted somewhere in the room. In her room the rules had the heading "We Decided." The rules were almost identical to
those she had posted herself, but she noticed that cooperation and mutual respect improved when the students
were involved in the discussion.

Many teachers have found that field trips are more
successful if they are discussed first in a class meeting.
Have the students discuss all the things that could go
wrong on the field trip to make it a bad experience and
decide on solutions to these potential problems. They
can then discuss what they need to do to make it a pleasant field trip.

Class meetings have also been helpful in making the
substitute's job easier. Have a discussion about substi-
tutes. Ask the students what they could do to "bug a
sub." After they discuss this, ask them how a substitute
might feel when being "bugged." It is amazing how
many students never consider the substitute's feelings.
Ask for ideas on how to make things pleasant for the
substitute. Then ask how many are willing to help instead
of hurt. When class meetings are a regular part of classroom procedure, student misbehavior is reduced when
there is a substitute because self-discipline and cooperation increases. When students forget, misbehavior is reported on the agenda.

How to End Class Meetings

When class meetings are effective, students often get so involved that they would like to continue beyond a reasonable time. This problem is eliminated if meetings are held just before lunch or recess. It is rare that students want to continue into lunch or recess time.

Enforcing Consequences

It is not necessary for the teacher to enforce the consequences decided upon by the group. The students will be very aware of what happens, and if another student should "forget," he or she will be reminded, or it will go back on the agenda.

Things Often Get Worse Before They Get Better

Remember this point so that you won't become discouraged. Students quite often don't trust that adults are really willing to listen to them and take them seriously. It may take some time for them to get used to this. At first they may try to use this new power to be hurtful and punishing, because this is the model they have been used to.

Keep your long-range goals in mind and maintain the courage to be imperfect. Many teachers have been tempted to quit before they make it through the rough part. Some probably do. Those who "hang in there" express their delight with all the benefits for themselves and their students as things get smoother.

It is suggested that you read this chapter several times because there is so much to learn in order to have successful class meetings. If you read it again after trying class meetings, you will probably understand many points that were missed on the first reading.

Group Exercises

Questions have been omitted for this chapter. It is suggested that as a group you discuss each of the questions and answers under the heading "Common Questions."

It is also suggested that you try to observe each other conducting class meetings. So much can be learned from watching someone else. You can also give each other valuable feedback. The "Class-Meeting Observation" form in the appendix is for this purpose.

Chapter Eight

FAMILY MEETINGS

When Jim and Betty married, they each brought three children to their newly blended family. The six children ranged in age from six to fourteen. Obviously, there were many adjustments to be made.

Betty was employed outside the home. She really enjoyed her new family and was anxious to get home to them after work—except for one problem. The first thing she would notice when she returned home was the mess. The children would come home from school and leave their books, sweaters, and shoes all over the house. To this they would add cookie crumbs, empty milk glasses, and toys.

Betty would start nagging and cajoling, "Why can't you pick up your things? You know it upsets me. I enjoy being with you, but I get so angry when I see all this mess that I forget about the joy." The children would pick up their things, but by then Betty was upset and displeased with them and with herself.

Betty finally put the problem on the agenda for their weekly, Monday-night family meeting. She admitted that it was her problem. It obviously didn't bother the children to have the house cluttered, but she asked that they help with her problem.

The children came up with a plan for a "safe-deposit box." This was to be a big cardboard box, which they would put in the garage. The rules were that anything that was left in the common rooms, such as the living room, family room, and kitchen, could be picked up by anyone who saw it and put in the safe-deposit box. They also decided it would have to stay there for a week before the owner could claim it.

The plan worked beautifully. The clutter problem was taken care of, and the safe-deposit box was jammed with things.

However, it caused some other problems, which tested the plan. If they hadn't stuck to the rules, the whole thing would have been ineffective. For instance, twelve-year-old David lost his school shoes. He looked everywhere and then remembered the safe-deposit box. Sure enough, that is where they were.

David wore his smelly, old tennis shoes to school; but the next day he lost those. He didn't have any other shoes, but the children insisted he couldn't take them out for a week.

David turned to Mother, who wisely said, "I'm sorry. I don't know what you are going to do, but I have to stick by the rules too." His helpful siblings finally came up with the solution of his bedroom slippers. David didn't have a better idea, so he wore his slippers to school for three days. After that week, he never left his shoes out again.

Then David's sister, eight-year-old Susan, lost her

coat. It was very difficult for Mom and Dad to stay out of these situations. After all, what kind of parents let their children go to school in their slippers and outside without a coat when the weather is so cold? They decided to forget about what other people might think and let Susan handle the problem by herself as David had. Susan wore two sweaters to school for a week.

The enlightening thing to Betty was how many of her own things disappeared into the safe-deposit box. She realized how much easier it was to see the clutter of others than to see her own.

Jim also "lost" some ties, a sport coat, and magazines. This plan worked because of the following concepts.

· The problem was shared in a family meeting.
· The children created the solution.
· Mom and Dad did not take responsibility when problems arose in carrying out the family's decision.
· The children enforced the rules because Mom and Dad stayed out of it.
· The rules applied to everyone in the family, including Mom and Dad.

Another family solved the same problem in almost the same way. In a family meeting, they decided on different rules for what they called the Disappear Box. Anyone who lost an item could retrieve it any time they wanted it, but they had to put a nickel in the Party Jar. When the jar filled up with nickels, which it did frequently, they would use the money for a family party of ice cream or pizza.

Parents can avoid most hassles with their children by suggesting that problems be put on the family-meeting agenda so that they can be solved—after a cooling-off period.

Family meetings can also be a very successful method of enhancing family cooperation and closeness. Their success, of course, depends on the same adult attitudes and skills that have been explained in previous chapters.

The chapter on class meetings should be read by parents, since many concepts that are important for successful group meetings have not been repeated in this chapter.

The format for family meetings is essentially the same as class meetings, except for six important differences:

1. Family meetings should be held once a week rather than once a day. After a time has been decided upon for family meetings, nothing should interfere. If friends call, tell them you will call back later. We unplug the phone. Do not skip a family meeting because you are busy or have something else to do. Your children will follow your lead in determining the importance of family meetings. Once the tradition has been effectively established, everyone will look forward to this opportunity for family togetherness.

2. Decisions should be made by consensus rather than a majority vote. If the family cannot come to a decision by consensus on an agenda item, it should be tabled until the next meeting, when it is likely that a consensus will be reached because of the additional cooling-off period and time to think of new ideas. A majority vote in a family meeting would accentuate a family division.

3. Family meetings should include a review of the next week's activities. This is especially important as the children grow older and become involved in many activities,

such as baby-sitting, sports, dates, lessons, and so on. Coordinating the calendar for car use and mutual convenience can be essential.

4. Family meetings should not end without planning a family fun activity during the coming week.

5. End the meeting by playing a game together or serving a dessert.

6. Sitting at a cleared table is conducive to staying on task for problem solving. The table does not seem to be the barrier for families that desks are in a classroom. Sitting informally in a living room or at the dinner table for family meetings is not as productive as sitting at a cleared table.

COMPONENTS OF THE FAMILY MEETING

Chairperson

This job should rotate. Children love to be the chairperson and can do a very good job after they reach the age of four or five. It is the chairperson's responsibility to call the meeting to order, start the compliments, begin the problem-solving sessions, and call on people who raise their hand.

Secretary

This job should also rotate among members of the family who are able to write. The secretary keeps notes of problems discussed and decisions made. (Reading old family-meeting journals can be more fun than looking at picture albums.)

Compliments

Begin by having each person give every other member of the family a compliment. This may be awkward at first if the children have the habit of putting each other down. If this is the case, spend some time discussing the kinds of things they could look for to compliment each other about. Parents can model this behavior by beginning with compliments for each member of the family. Also, if you see something nice going on between the children, remind them to remember it for a compliment. You might even suggest that they write it in on the agenda so they will remember.

Mrs. Stover shared the following incident that occurred when her family began giving compliments in their family meetings. Six-year-old Tammy volunteered to go first. She complimented her Mom and her Dad with joy and ease. When she came to her nine-year-old brother, Marcus, she paused and said, "This is really hard." Mr. and Mrs. Stover encouraged her to do it anyway. She finally thought of something she could compliment Marcus for, then added, "But he is also mean to me."

Her parents admonished, "No buts." When it was Marcus's turn, he was not any more enthusiastic about complimenting Tammy, but he did it. Mrs. Stover said that now they compliment each other with ease and added, "It is amazing to hear siblings saying nice things about each other when their pattern had been nothing but put-downs.

Gratitude

We alternate between compliments and sharing what we are grateful for. Having each family member share one thing he or she is grateful for helps us remember and appreciate so much that we usually take for granted.

The Agenda

The refrigerator seems to be the most popular place for family agendas; it is so simple to use a magnet to hang a piece of paper on the front or side.

Discuss agenda items in chronological order, so that a decision does not need to be made about which item is the most important.

Problem Solving

Discuss logical consequences with the children as outlined in chapter 7. The Three Rs of Logical Consequences should be used to solve many problems in family meetings, just as they are in class meetings. In family meetings, however, consequences must be agreed upon by consensus.

Many problems can be solved by agreeing on a plan of action that may not include logical consequences.

Planning Activities

Family members are more willing to cooperate when they have participated equally in planning events they will all enjoy.

Weekly activities and vacations are more successful

when the whole family participates in a discussion of possible conflicts and how to avoid them. As in the following example shared by my husband, Barry Nelsen.

"Let's take the kids to Hawaii," my wife said.

"Are you kidding? They will make life miserable for all of us," I replied.

Little did I know that six weeks later I would return from one of my most enjoyable family outings in many years. The reason for the success of this trip was family meetings.

We have family meetings every Sunday night. Each member of the family is treated with respect, and every opinion is heard and discussed.

During a family meeting several weeks before our trip to Hawaii, I told the kids that Mom and I were going to Hawaii soon, and asked if they would like to go with us. Pandemonium broke loose. After we convinced them to calm down, Mom said, "If we take you to Hawaii, it needs to be fun for Dad and me too. If you fight with each other, or argue about every little thing we ask you to do, it won't be fun for us."

The kids promised to be angels! I had heard that before, and knew we needed more than promises. We decided to brainstorm and list the things that make life miserable for parents on vacation with kids.

"What about things that make life miserable for kids?" Mark interrupted. We all agreed that was a fair question. Mom listed the potential problems in two columns: hassles for parents, and hassles for kids.

The parent hassle list included: begging for money, eating nothing but junk food, fighting with each other, arguing with us, not picking up their stuff, not carrying their own bags, running off without telling us where they are going, staying up too late, and not wanting to go to some of the places we want to go. The kid hassle list included: eating at fancy restaurants, wearing fancy clothes, both sleeping in the same bed, not enough money, being told what they can or can't buy, and not getting a window seat on the airplane. The agreed upon solutions were: the kids would save as much money as they could; we would add a specific amount (and no more), they would divide the total amount by seven days and have us give them that amount every day, we would not tell them how to spend their money and would not give them any more when it was gone; they agreed to be responsible for their own luggage and wouldn't pack more than they wanted to carry; Mark would take a sleeping bag and sleep on the floor if the only other choice was one bed for the two of them; they would eat at McDonalds when we ate at nicer restaurants; they would take turns at a window seat during takeoff and landing, they agreed not to fight, and to always let us know where they were going.

"What happens if they forget and start to fight?" I asked.

"How about giving us a secret signal?" Mark suggested.

"Good idea," Mom said. "If I hear you fighting, I'll pull my earlobe to give you a silent reminder that you agreed not to fight."

"That goes for you too, Dad," Mark chimed in.

"What do you mean by that?" I asked indignantly.

"When you start to lose your temper with me or Mary, is it okay if I pull on my ear to signal you?"

That little wise guy, I thought. But then I reflected and agreed, "Good idea, Son."

A week before we left, and three meetings later, our lists had grown. There was an atmosphere of excitement and cooperation throughout the family. The kids were getting ahead in their schoolwork, and money was being saved diligently.

One of the first conflicts came when Mark wanted to take his skateboard along. I explained all the problems it might cause on crowded Waikiki streets, the difficulty he would have carrying it along with his baggage. Since a feeling of cooperation had been established, he agreed to leave it home without arguing.

The two-hour drive to San Francisco to catch the plane turned out to be three hours. Mary started to whine about being thirsty while we were in a traffic jam on the Bay Bridge. When we reminded her that we had already talked about this sort of hassle, she quickly decided she could wait until we got to the airport. Another victory for family meetings!

The hotel room in Honolulu had two double beds. We were glad we had taken Mark's sleeping bag to avoid arguments.

Thanks to family meetings, we had a great time! There were a few hassles, but they were solved quickly with reminders of our agreements. The kids got lost once. We had a family meeting to decide how to avoid that possibility in the future. We decided we would go back to the last place we had seen each other together, and wait for the others to come back and find us. The kids also memorized our hotel and address so they would have that information for a policeman if they got lost again.

The closeness we felt as a family was an even greater experience than the trip to Hawaii.

Two weeks after we got home, our oldest son called from Florida to say he was getting married in two months. "Let's take the kids." I said.

Planning for Family Fun

Planning weekly family fun activities is an important part of family meetings, but it is an area neglected by many families.

It is so easy to think about how nice it would be to have a happy family that does fun and exciting things together. The catch is that so many families hope it will "just happen" without any effort on their part. It doesn't happen unless you do something to make it happen. To make it happen you must "plan and do."

The first step in *planning* is to give each member of the family a sheet of paper with the following headings:

FUN THINGS TO DO

TOGETHER AS A FAMILY		HUSBAND AND WIFE		ALONE	
Free	For $	Free	For $	Free	For $

Have all family members work on their sheets for at least a week so that they have plenty of time to add everything they can think of.

The second step in planning is to have a family meeting for sharing your ideas. Get a calendar and decide which days or nights you can set aside for family fun. Decide when you can spend money and how much, and when you should plan free things. Then work for a consensus as to which of the fun things you want to do on each of the designated days or nights for the next three months. Plot each decision on the calendar.

The essential step for *doing* is simply to follow your planned calendar.

Our family used the "Fun Things to Do" sheets for *planning and doing* a family activity as follows: We decided that every Saturday night would be date night. The first Saturday, Mom and Mark do something together, while Dad and Mary are together. The first Saturday of the next month, they switch so that Mom and Mary spend special time together, while Dad and Mark have their special time. The second and fourth Saturdays of the month are date nights for Mom and Dad alone. The third Saturday we all do something together as a whole family.

We use the "Fun Things to Do" sheets for planning and doing on our Saturday date nights.

Discussion of Chores

Discuss chores at a family meeting so that children can help solve the problems of getting them done. They are more cooperative when they can voice their feelings and be part of the planning and choosing.

At one family meeting we listed all the chores done by Mom and Dad (including full-time employment) in an effort to eliminate "How come I have to do everything?" whenever we asked one of our children to do something. We then listed all the chores that could be done by children. When they saw the comparison between what we ask of them and what we do, they were impressed. We then put the chores they could do on slips of paper that could be drawn from a jar each week. Each child now draws four chores each week. There is a new drawing every week so that one child is never stuck with the same chore all the time, such as the garbage.

This is not a magic solution. We find that the problem of getting chores done is put on our agenda at least once a month. Even though we need to keep working on it, we feel we get much greater cooperation by handling the problem through family meetings than any other way we have tried. We achieve great responsibility for a while. When it starts to slack off, we put it on the agenda and get renewed cooperation. Dealing with the problem of chores every three or four weeks is far preferable to hassling over them every day.

SOME SPECIAL PROBLEMS

Small Children

Some families find that children under four years of age are disruptive during the problem-solving part of family meetings. In my own family, we used to wait until babies and toddlers were in bed to have family meetings.

As soon as the children were old enough, we included them for some parts of the family meeting. Three-year-old children love to participate in a game of Hide the

Button or Hide and Seek followed by dessert. They can even learn to give compliments. By the age of four, children are wonderfully creative at problem solving and are ready for full participation.

Teenagers

Power struggles and revenge cycles have often become well established in many homes by the time children become teenagers. Family meetings can change these patterns dramatically, but it takes special groundwork to get them established. The first requirement is enough humility from parents to admit that what they have been doing has not been working. The second step is to admit this to the teenagers.

Mr. Lyon shared how he won his teenagers over. He told them, "I have really been going down the wrong path with you guys. I have yelled at you about cooperating when what I really meant was 'do it my way.' No wonder you didn't want to. I admire your perceptiveness in not falling for that. I would really like to start over, and I need your help. I've heard about the effectiveness of family meetings, where families sit down together and solve problems with mutual respect for the validity of everyone's opinions. I'll need your help to remind me when I start my old habits."

Mr. Lyon's teenagers were stunned speechless by this new behavior on the part of their father. Mr. Lyon was wise enough to quickly add, "I know this is really new to you. Why don't you think about it and let me know tomorrow if you would be willing to work with me on this."

Mr. Lyon charmingly shared with his parent study

group, "How could they resist?" They didn't. Mr. Lyon continued to share many wonderful experiences he had in his family meetings and how much he was now enjoying his teenagers—hassles and all.

Single Parents

The family-meeting process is equally effective for single-parent families. A family can consist of one parent and one child, or one parent and several children. It is a myth that children are deprived if they don't have two parents. Many great people have been raised by a single parent. Single-parent families simply provide different opportunities.

A parent's attitude is very important. If you feel guilty about your children having only a single full-time parent, they will sense that a tragedy is taking place and will act accordingly. If you accept the fact that you are doing the best you can under the circumstances and are moving toward success rather than failure, children will sense this and act accordingly.

Family meetings are a good way to convey positive feelings to children and to get them involved in solutions rather than manipulation.

Mrs. Doherty and Mrs. Latimer are single parents of one child each, who all live together. They shared that they could not have survived without their weekly family meetings. Once a week they were able to talk about and solve all the problems that are typical between roommates, as well as those between parents and children and siblings.

For many families, weekly meetings are a family tradition, providing children with a sense of well-being, self-confidence, significance, and belonging. They also provide family fun, mutual respect, problem-solving experiences, and happy memories.

QUESTIONS FOR REVIEW OF CHAPTER 8

1. By way of review from other chapters, what are some of the basic concepts and adult attitudes that are important for family meetings to be successful?

2. What are some of the skills children will learn by participating in family meetings?

3. What are six differences between family meetings and class meetings, and why should they be different?

4. What is the value of having each person compliment every other member of the family?

5. What is the value of having children share what they are grateful for?

6. What are the five concepts that contributed to the success of the safe-deposit box plan?

7. Discuss how to achieve a hassle-free vacation.

8. What is the best way to teach children cooperation and responsibility regarding chores?

9. Why is it just as important for single-parent families to have family meetings?

10. Imagine and discuss some of the benefits you might realize from trying the "plan and do" program.

Chapter Nine

PUTTING IT ALL TOGETHER

Most of the principles described in this book require the understanding and application of more than one basic concept and several adult attitudes. When we put them all together, we have a greater chance for success in helping children lay the foundation to develop the characteristics that will serve them well throughout their lives.

All the following techniques help children learn responsibility, self-discipline, and cooperation. They all require the support of other techniques, plus attitudes of love, understanding, friendliness, firmness with kindness, and mutual respect.

THE BATHROOM TECHNIQUE

The value of a cooling-off period has been mentioned several times. This usually involves some type of temporary withdrawal from the conflict situation.

The best place for parents to withdraw is to the bathroom. Dreikurs is well known for this technique. He suggested the bathroom because it is the only room in many houses with a lock on the door.

If you find the need to spend a lot of time cooling off in the bathroom, you might like to make it as comfortable for yourself as possible with books, magazines, and a stereo.

A respectful attitude is very important in using any type of cooling-off period. It is helpful to discuss the value of such periods with children during a family meeting or individually. Explain that the purpose is to take time out to make yourself feel better, since problems cannot be solved respectfully at the time of conflict. Reassure children that when everyone feels better, the problem will be solved with respect and cooperation.

THE NOVEL TECHNIQUE

Since teachers cannot leave children alone in the classroom, one way they can withdraw is to sit down and read a novel during times of conflict. (Teachers who have tried this find it is very effective, but many teachers do not feel comfortable with this technique. Try it if it fits your style.)

The first step is to tell the children your plan. Let them know that your job is to teach—theirs is to learn. If they are not willing to do their job, you cannot do yours. Tell them that from now on, whenever they are being disruptive so that you are unable to teach, you will sit down and read your novel. They can let you know when they are ready to do their job so that you can do yours.

The reason some teachers do not like this technique is

that they can't stand the testing period, when things get worse before they get better. The children will usually be very disruptive as they test their new freedom. However, before too long, the children will settle down and let the teacher know they are ready to learn.

This technique is effective only for teachers who have earned the admiration and respect of the children because they are well prepared and effective. It is also most effective with children in elementary grades. It would be disastrous with teenagers, who are more concerned with peer approval than adult approval.

Mr. Rasmussen, a special education teacher of fourth-, fifth-, and sixth-grade students, received permission from his principal to leave the room when his students were being disruptive. He first explained to the students that he would leave when they were not ready to learn. They were instructed to come get him in the teacher's lounge when they were ready.

That same day the students got so noisy they could not hear him unless he raised his voice. He took his coffee cup and left the room.

Mr. Rasmussen got very nervous while he was sitting in the teacher's lounge. He was not at all sure this would work. His imagination went wild as he considered the things the children could be doing in the room. When they had not come to get him after thirty minutes, he began to wonder if he would lose his teaching contract.

After forty-five minutes, one of the students came to the teacher's lounge to tell Mr. Rasmussen they were ready for him to come back and teach. He was amazed at how cooperative the children were for the next few days.

The next time the students became disruptive, Mr.

Rasmussen took his coffee cup off the shelf. Immediately the children settled down and said they were ready.

After hearing this story, another special education teacher tried it. She reported that her students came to her in twenty minutes with a signed petition stating they were ready to cooperate.

Another teacher forgot to tell her students where they could find her. They went to the office and had her paged over the intercom when they were ready.

I'm not advocating you try this if there are strict rules in your school against it. Some principals will give permission for this kind of risk taking.

THE ISOLATION TECHNIQUE

It was mentioned in a previous chapter that isolation can be a good logical consequence for misbehaving children if it is requested in a kind and firm manner, followed by the encouraging instructions to come back when the child is ready.

The bathroom and novel techniques are usually better, because you are deciding what you will do instead of what you are going to try and make the child do (a technique that will be explained later). But many parents and teachers like to use the isolation technique instead of the bathroom technique, because they feel it is too inconvenient for them to withdraw to the bathroom if they are busy with a task, such as fixing dinner or teaching a class. (However, sometimes a short period of inconvenience is a small price to pay in order to help children learn responsibility and cooperation.)

Mrs. James started putting Ann in her bedroom for

misbehavior when she was fourteen months old. She would leave her there for about three minutes before bringing her back out. If Ann started misbehaving again, she would immediately be put back in her room for another three minutes. Ann soon made the connection. The reason Mrs. James would get her in three minutes was that Ann was too young to be able to say when she was ready.

By the time Ann was two, she could say, "I'm ready to come out." Mrs. James had her role-play how to say this in a happy voice to show she was ready.

When Ann would misbehave, such as whining or jumping on the furniture, Mrs. James would take her to her room and shut the door. Ann would cry and scream and sometimes kick on the door for a while before she remembered to knock and say she was ready to come out.

By the time she was three, Mrs. James would give her a choice: "Would you like to behave, or would you like to go to your room?" If Ann continued her misbehavior, Mrs. James would then say, "I see you have decided to go to your room. Would you like to go by yourself, or would you like me to help you?" If Ann didn't take either choice, Mrs. James would say, "I see you have chosen to let me help you." She would then kindly and firmly take Ann to her room and say, "You can stay in your room with the door open or shut until you are ready to come out." Ann would usually come out while she was still crying. Mrs. James would then say, "I see you have decided to have the door shut. You can stay in your room with the door shut or locked until you are ready to come out." If Ann came out before she was ready, Mrs. James would say, "I see you have decided to have the door locked. Let me know when you are ready to come out."

By the time Ann was four, she was very familiar with this routine. When she misbehaved, she would either go to her room by herself or with kind and firm assistance. Sometimes she would cry for a while before indicating she was ready to come out. Other times she would simply play in her room for a while or fall asleep.

Mrs. James learned to use the bathroom technique when she had surgery and did not have the strength to assist Ann to her bedroom when she misbehaved. One day Ann was whining, so Mrs. James hobbled down the hall to the bathroom. Ann followed her and started pounding on the door crying, "I want you to come out." After a few minutes Mrs. James heard Ann try to control some involuntary sobs before she said in a happy voice, "I'm ready for you to come out."

An important concept to review here is: Where did we ever get the crazy idea that in order to make children do better, first we have to make them feel worse. Most adults have the mistaken idea that the whole point of sending children to their rooms is to make them suffer. "You go to your room and think about what you did." The tone of voice usually implies, "And you suffer."

One parent even complained, "It doesn't do any good to send my child to his room, he enjoys it."

I said, "Great. That will produce better results."

In fact, I suggest to parents that they teach their children during a calm, happy time. "When I send you to your room for misbehaving, go into your room and do something to make yourself feel better. You can read a book, play with your toys, listen to music, or take a nap. Then, when you feel better, come on out and we will work on a solution."

Many parents object, "But isn't that rewarding misbehavior?"

It could work out as a reward for misbehavior if a parent does not follow through with problem solving when everyone is feeling good.

Sometimes it may be parents who need to go to their rooms and do something to make themselves feel good enough to work on solutions with dignity and respect.

DECIDE WHAT YOU WILL DO, NOT WHAT YOU WILL MAKE CHILDREN DO

The potential danger in asking a child to go to his room (or any other request) is that you may be inviting a power struggle if he refuses. This is especially true with older children. The possibility is eliminated when you allow children to learn from the natural or logical consequences of what you decide to do, rather than what you try to make them do.

Bonnie married a widower with six children. The oldest was eight years old and the youngest were two-year-old twins. The mother of these children had died in childbirth when the twins were born. You can imagine how difficult it was to find a baby-sitter for six children, including baby twins. Even those who were desperate for a job did not stay long, so the children had not had the stability of consistent discipline before Bonnie became their new mother. This was especially evident during mealtime, which was a terrible ordeal because the children would fight, argue, and throw food at each other.

Bonnie had taught Adlerian/Dreikursian principles before she had a chance to practice them. Now she had her chance.

The first thing Bonnie did was hold a family meeting. She did not even discuss their mealtime behavior. She simply asked them to decide how much time they needed to eat their food after it was on the table. They talked it over and decided fifteen minutes was plenty of time. (They forgot to consider how much time it takes to fight, argue, and throw food.)

They all willingly agreed to a family rule that dinner would be served at 6:00 P.M. and the table cleared at 6:15.

The next evening Bonnie and her husband ignored the fighting while they ate their food. (I know how difficult this is for parents to do. We will discuss why it is important at the end of this example.) At 6:15 Bonnie cleared the table. The children protested that they were still hungry and were not through eating. Bonnie kindly and firmly replied, "I am just following the rule we agreed on. I am sure you can make it until breakfast." She then sat in front of the refrigerator with a novel and earplugs for the rest of the evening.

The next night was a repeat of the previous night as the children tested to see if their new mother was "for real." By the third night they knew she was, and they were so busy eating that they did not have time to fight, argue, or throw food.

There is a lovely sequel to this story. Six years later I had the opportunity to stay with these children while their parents took a weekend vacation. They were so responsible and capable that I did not lift a finger the whole weekend.

The children prepared all the meals and did their chores without any interference from me. They showed me their meal and chore plan. They planned all their menus for a month during the first family meeting of the month. They all had a night to cook, except Mom (who did all the shopping) and the oldest boy (who had football practice).

I asked them if things always ran so smoothly. One of the girls told me that they used to have a rule that whoever cooked did not clean the kitchen. This caused problems because those who had the cleanup chore always complained about the messy cooks. They decided to change the rule so that the cook also cleaned the kitchen. This solved the complaints and gave everyone a longer break before it was their turn again.

This example illustrates several points that are important in making the technique successful:

· Let the children know what you are going to do. If possible, get their agreement as to what will be done under certain circumstances.

· Use actions, not words. When children test your new plan, the fewer words you use, the better. *Keep your mouth shut and act.*

· The few words you do use should be stated in a kind and friendly manner.

· Ignore the temptation to become involved in a power struggle or revenge cycle. Children will do their best to get you sucked in to your usual response.

· When following through with your plan, it may seem that you are letting the children "get away with something" while you ignore their misbehavior. It is true that punishment would get more immediate results, but this technique helps children develop responsibility for the future (long-range results).

· Things will get worse before they get better. Be consistent with your new plan of action and children will learn a new response ability. (The play on words is intended.)

Following are some other examples of deciding what you will do instead of what you will make children do:

Don't try to make children put their dirty clothes in the hamper. Simply decide that you will wash only the clothes that are in the hamper. Children will soon learn from the natural consequence of not having clean clothes when they want them.

Don't nag at children to clean up the kitchen. Simply refuse to cook until the kitchen is clean. Think how much fun you can have reading a good novel while you wait. At first the children might think it is just great to fix their own peanut butter sandwiches whenever they are hungry. This gets old after a while, and children soon see that cooperation is a two-way street, if they want to enjoy the finer meals of life.

Do not distort this technique into a power struggle or revenge cycle. Some parents misunderstand this concept and try to use it to bully or shame children into doing what they want them to do or to "get even" with them for not doing what they "should" do.

The idea is to become unconcerned with what children do in these situations. In other words, don't be concerned if your child chooses to wear dirty clothes instead of taking responsibility for putting them in the hamper. Don't be concerned if your children would prefer to eat peanut butter sandwiches instead of cleaning up the kitchen so that you will cook. Enjoy the vacation from the kitchen.

This is a technique that is extremely effective for those parents and teachers who feel comfortable using it. They use it in conjunction with other techniques, such as family or class meetings, taking time for training, and encouragement. Those who cannot stand to become unconcerned can use other techniques.

EMOTIONAL WITHDRAWAL

I have discussed the value of a cooling-off period before trying to solve problems rationally. The purpose is to withdraw from the situation until the emotional conflict is over, instead of getting into power struggles or revenge cycles. The bathroom technique or isolation is suggested because most adults and children have difficulty cooling off until they leave the area of conflict. It would not be necessary to leave the area if we could withdraw *emotionally* and avoid becoming involved in a contest.

Bonnie and her husband (mentioned earlier in this chapter) had to withdraw emotionally in order to be able to ignore the children's misbehavior at the dinner table while they followed their new plan of action.

Mrs. Valdez, a third-grade teacher, invited me to observe her class meeting. I arrived early and had the opportunity to witness how effectively she used emotional withdrawal.

It was time to change from a math activity to reading. The children were becoming noisy and disruptive. I saw Mrs. Valdez stare at the back wall as though she had gone into a trance. The children noticed also and started whispering. "She is counting." The word was passed, and soon the children were sitting quietly at attention.

Later, in the teacher's room, I asked Mrs. Valdez,

"How high do you count, and what do you do after you get there?"

She said, "I'm not really counting. I have just decided I can't teach until the children are quiet, so I might as well take a break. Since I stare at the back wall while I'm waiting, the children assume I'm looking at the clock and counting. They never seemed to hear me when I nagged at them to settle down, but they get quiet very quickly since I have decided not to teach until they are ready."

Another teacher uses counting and logical consequences. She writes the amount of time that was wasted on the board and has the class make up that time during recess or after school. This is much different than writing names on the board to single certain children out for humiliation and punishment.

Emotional withdrawal does not mean withdrawing from the child. It does mean withdrawing from a conflict-producing situation. All withdrawal techniques should be followed with encouragement, training, redirecting, or problem-solving activities after the cooling-off period.

AVOIDING MORNING HASSLES

The following story illustrates several concepts, attitudes, and techniques previously discussed, as well as the importance of establishing routines.

Mornings at DaniRie's house are usually very hectic. She finds this an excellent time to keep Mother busy with her. The scene usually goes something like this:

"DaniRie, will you please get up! . . . This is the last time I'm going to call you! . . . How should I know where your books are? Where did you leave them? . . . You're

still not dressed and the bus will be here in five minutes!
. . . DaniRie, I mean it, this is absolutely the last time I'm
going to drive you when you miss the bus. You have got
to learn to be more responsible."

If this sounds familiar and you believe the old adage,
"Misery loves company," you may find some consolation
in knowing this scene is repeated in millions of homes
every morning.

This is not the last time Mother will drive DaniRie to
school when she misses the bus, a fact DaniRie is well
aware of. She has heard this threat many times and knows
it is meaningless.

Mother is right, DaniRie should learn to be more
responsible. But through morning scenes like this,
Mother is actually training DaniRie to be more and more
irresponsible. Instead of giving her practice in responsibility, she is giving her practice in calculated manipulation. Mother is the one who is responsible when she is
constantly reminding DaniRie of everything she needs to
do. DaniRie will learn responsible behavior when
Mother stays out of the way and allows her to experience
the consequences of being late. She may have to walk to
school if she misses her bus; or her teacher may have her
make up the time she misses.

Morning hassles can be avoided through taking time
for training, involving children in planning, establishing
routines, and logical consequences.

AVOIDING BEDTIME HASSLES

The following story demonstrates how avoiding morning
hassles is also dependent on some routines that take place

the night before as part of the routines that help avoid bedtime hassles.

Mrs. Felix took time to train Matthew to dress himself when he was two years old. She purchased the kind of clothes that are easy to pull on and off. She then went through the procedure with Matthew several times. Once she was sure he knew how, she never allowed him to retrain her into doing it for him.

Since Matthew went to a morning preschool, Mrs. Felix got him up early enough to have plenty of time for dressing and eating so that Mr. Felix could take him to school on his way to work. She explained to Matthew that if he didn't get dressed on time, she would put his clothes in a paper bag so that he could get dressed in the car on his way to school—an excellent logical consequence.

They established the following routines beginning the night before school. At 7:00 P.M. Matthew would get into his pajamas before his bedtime snack.

Next came the bathroom routine. Matthew's family enjoyed the routine (tradition) of taking turns getting out everyone's toothbrush and putting toothpaste on them. As each family member went to the bathroom and discovered the toothpaste already on their brush, they would sing out, "Thank you."

Then Mom or Dad would take Matthew into his room and have him pick out the clothes he wanted to wear the next day so that he could have them all ready for morning. (This routine avoids the hassle of trying to decide what to wear in the morning when time pressures make it so inviting for a child to demand something he can't find or that is in the dirty-clothes hamper. As he grows older, he will also learn to lay out his books, coat, and everything else he will need in the morning.) Mom or

Dad would then talk to him about his day, read him a story, and tuck him into bed with a goodnight kiss.

Matthew had his own clock radio that woke him up in the morning. He would get up, get dressed, and come to the kitchen to help with breakfast. (In the Felix family, everyone has a job to help with breakfast. Their jobs change each week at their family meeting.) Matthew's favorite job is scrambling the eggs—a job two-year-old children do very well after a "time for training."

If Matthew finishes his routines before it is time to leave, he can then turn on the TV and watch a few cartoons.

One cold, rainy day, Matthew dawdled and was not ready when it was time to leave. His father took naked Matthew under one arm, his clothes in a bag under the other arm, and walked out into the rain to the car. Matthew cried all the way to his school, but Dad was able to ignore it. When Matthew got to school, his teacher (who also believes in these principles) kindly said to him, "Oh, I see you didn't get dressed yet. Take your clothes into the changing room and come out as soon as you are dressed."

From then on Matthew was usually dressed on time. A few times his mother would notice him dawdling and say, "It looks as if you have decided to get dressed in the car." Matthew didn't like that idea, so he would hurry and finish getting dressed. Mother could have eliminated taking responsibility for even these reminders by allowing Matthew to experience the logical consequences again.

QUALITY BEDTIME SHARING

One reason children give their parents such a hard time at bedtime is because they can *feel* that their parents are trying to get rid of them. It is understandable that at the end of a long day, parents look forward to peace and quiet. Instead they usually experience the frustration of bedtime hassles. Spending a few minutes of *quality bedtime sharing* is important for helping to eliminate frustrations.

When children sense that you are in a hurry to get away from them, they feel discouraged about belonging. They then misbehave by demanding drinks, bathroom privileges, or crying about fears. When they sense you really enjoy being with them for a few minutes of quality sharing, they feel a sense of belonging and don't need to misbehave.

Sharing the saddest and the happiest events of the day works very well to help children feel content. A fringe benefit is that parents enjoy it too.

AVOIDING MEALTIME HASSLES

Mealtimes have become such a battleground that you would think children would rather be hungry than eat. It is not that they would rather be hungry than eat, but they would rather feel *powerful* than eat. It is almost impossible to make children eat, but that doesn't keep parents from trying. Many times parents think they have succeeded, only to have their children vomit their food up again.

Mrs. Williams served four-year-old Sara oatmeal for breakfast. Sara wouldn't eat it, in spite of her mother's scolding. Mrs. Williams put it in the refrigerator and served it to Sara for lunch. She still wouldn't eat it—so she got it for dinner. Mrs. Williams was an authoritarian mother who dominated Sara in many areas. Sara did not know how to "win," except during mealtime. This one area where she could feel independent and powerful was so important that she was sacrificing her body. Sara got rickets.

Mrs. Williams took Sara to the doctor, who guessed what was happening. He was a wise man and advised, "Leave her alone! Put nutritious food on the table, eat your own food, and mind your own business. Talk about pleasant things or else keep your mouth shut."

Mrs. Williams felt very bad about what had happened. The only reason she had harassed Sara about eating was that she loved her and mistakenly thought that was the best way to get her to eat and be healthy. As with many controlling methods when used with today's children, it had backfired and she had achieved the opposite of what she wanted. She took the doctor's advice and stopped the war over eating. Sara never became a hearty eater (she is a very small-boned child), but she ate enough to overcome the rickets and stay healthy.

It is interesting to talk to people who were raised during the Depression of the 1930s. They say that the only mealtime problem they had was, "Will there be enough food?" No one cared if one person chose not to eat. That would just mean there would be more for someone else. Children did not develop eating problems in that kind of atmosphere.

Getting children involved in planning and solutions is the best way to avoid mealtime problems. Take time during a family meeting to plan the meals for the following week.

The Ainge family brings a sheet of paper to their family meetings with the following headings: Main Dish, Vegetable, Salad, and Dessert. Together they fill in the columns for each day of the week. This creates an atmosphere of cooperation. When they have all been in on the planning, they are more willing to eat what someone else has chosen, because they have also had some choices.

The Ainge family also does the shopping together. They divide the shopping list into different sections of the grocery store. Each member of the family takes a different section. They enjoy trying to beat their time records. The children learn a lot about shopping, while having fun together to get a chore done. It is easy to see why this family does not have "war games" at the dinner table. They have been encouraged to use their "power" to contribute, cooperate, and enjoy each other.

STAYING OUT OF CHILDREN'S FIGHTS

The best way to train your children to fight is to keep getting involved in their fights. Parents have a difficult time believing that the main reason children fight is to get them involved, until they stay out of the arguments and experience the drastic reduction in fighting.

Most parents recognize the typical pattern of sibling fights based on birth order. The oldest child is usually the most "bugable," and the youngest child usually gets the greatest payoff for getting Mother involved. Thus, the youngest does something to provoke the oldest. This provocation could be anything from making a face at the oldest, to disturbing something in her room.

When the oldest bites the bait and goes after the youngest, there is a loud scream of protest to Mother from the youngest. Mother becomes involved by scolding the oldest. When the oldest is able to convince her that the youngest started it, Mother replies with, "I don't care what he has done. You are the oldest, and you should know better."

If Mother would notice the look of triumph on the youngest child's face, she would gain much insight into the purpose (mistaken goal) of the behavior. Mother is collaborating in their training to fight as a way of seeking attention, power, or revenge. She reinforces the children's mistaken beliefs about how to find belonging and significance.

Mrs. Reeder decided to stay out of her children's fights. She chose a conflict-free time and explained to them that she really didn't like getting involved in their fights and that from now on she was sure they could figure out ways to solve their own problems. During a family meeting they discussed the four problem-solving steps outlined in chapter 10.

The next day Mrs. Reeder was walking down the hall and happened to see seven-year-old Troy hit five-year-old Shaun on the head with a cap gun. She felt she couldn't ignore that and went charging into the bedroom to stop the fight. As a flashback, she realized that when Shaun was hit, he fell back on the bed and mildly complained to Troy, "That hurt." Then Shaun saw his mother and he let out a loud cry of protest. Mrs. Reeder realized she had been hooked and quickly turned around and went to the bathroom and locked the door. Both children followed her and started banging on the door, each wanting to tell his side of the story.

As Mrs. Reeder sat in the bathroom listening to the boys banging on the door and arguing about who started it, she thought, "Dreikurs is crazy! This isn't working!" However, she stuck it out a little longer so that she could report back to her study group what happened. The children soon stopped pounding on the door and went away.

Mrs. Reeder continued to stay out of their fights by telling them "I'm sure you can solve your own problems," whenever they came to her with a complaint. The family continued to discuss possible solutions to problems during family meetings.

Mrs. Reeder knew this technique had been effective when, about a month later, she overheard her four-year-old daughter, Colleen, say to Troy, "I'm going to tell Mom."

Troy replied, "She will just tell you to solve your own problem." (Colleen must have known Troy was right, because she didn't tell Mom.)

Mrs. Reeder reported that fighting among her children diminished by about 75 percent. The remaining 25 percent of fights were much milder and quickly solved.

There are circumstances when staying out of fights may be difficult or inadvisable:

· Some adults find it almost impossible to become unconcerned, even though they intellectually believe it to be the best thing to do.

· When children are very young, they may do serious damage to each other, such as a two-year-old hitting a six-month-old on the head with a toy firetruck. (Many adults use this excuse to get involved in the fights of older children.) If older children really want to hurt each other, they will do it when adults are not around. Adults should not assume the protective role with older children, unless they want it twenty-four hours a day.

· Teachers are responsible for student safety and cannot stay out of fights.

* * *

Some parents don't believe children fight mostly for the parents' benefit. They argue that their children fight even when they are not around. I always ask, "How do you know they fight when you are not around?"

They grin sheepishly as they admit, "Because they make sure I find out. Sometimes they even call me at work to get me involved. I can see now they are still trying to make me judge, jury, and executioner—of the other guy."

If you decide to become involved in fights, the most effective way is to "put your children in the same boat."

Do not take sides or try to decide who is at fault. Chances are you wouldn't be right, because you never see everything that goes on. "Right" is always a matter of opinion. What seems right to you will surely seem unfair from at least one child's point of view. If you feel you must get involved to stop fights, don't become judge, jury, and executioner. Instead, put them in the same boat and treat them the same.

Mrs. Hamilton noticed two-year-old Marilyn hitting eight-month-old Marjorie. Mrs. Hamilton felt that Marjorie had not done anything to provoke Marilyn, but she still put them both in their separate rooms and said, "Come out when you are ready to stop fighting."

We can't know for sure if Marjorie provoked Marilyn (innocently or purposefully). If she did, reprimanding Marilyn would not only be unfair, but it would teach Marjorie a good way to get Mother on her side. If she did not provoke Marilyn, reprimanding Marilyn (because she is the oldest) would teach Marjorie the possibility of getting special attention by provoking Marilyn. Marilyn might then adopt the mistaken belief that she is most significant as the "bad" child.

Another way to put children in the same boat is to give them both the same choice. "You can either stop fighting or go outside to settle your fight."

As children get older, fighting can be discussed at family meetings so that children can be involved in solutions.

When adults refuse to get involved in children's fights or put them in the same boat by giving them the same consequences for fighting, the biggest motive for fighting is eliminated.

NONVERBAL SIGNALS

Most of the techniques discussed so far in this chapter are forms of nonverbal signals. They all incorporate other important concepts and attitudes, such as allowing for a cooling-off period and being kind and firm at the same time. They stress action rather than words. When words are necessary, the fewer the better.

It is very effective to involve children in a problem-solving session, where you decide on a plan that includes a nonverbal signal in order to give adults additional help in learning to *keep their mouths shut.*

Mr. Perry, a principal, decided to attend a parent study group at his school. He made it clear to the group that he was attending as a parent who would like to learn some skills to use with his own children.

One night he asked the group to help him solve the problem of getting his son, Mike, to take out the garbage. Mike always agreed to do it, but never did without constant reminders.

The group gave Mr. Perry several suggestions, such as

turning the television off until it was done or giving Mike
a choice as to when he would do it. One parent suggested
to try the nonverbal signal of turning Mike's empty plate
over at the dinner table if he forgot to take the garbage
out before dinner. Mr. Perry decided to try this.

First, the family discussed the problem at a family
meeting. Mike again reaffirmed that he would do it. Mrs.
Perry said, "We appreciate your willingness to help, but
we also realize how easy it is to forget. Would it be okay
with you if we use a nonverbal signal so that we can stop
nagging?"

Mike wanted to know what kind of signal.

Mr. Perry explained the idea of turning his empty
plate over at the dinner table. If he came to the table and
saw his plate turned over, that would remind him. He
could then empty the garbage before coming to the
table. Mike said, "That is okay with me."

It was eight days before Mike forgot to empty the
garbage. (When children are involved in a problem-solving discussion, they usually cooperate for a while before
testing the plan.) When he came to the table and saw his
plate turned over, Mike started having a temper tantrum.
He whined, "I'm hungry! I'll take the garbage out later!
This is really dumb!"

I'm sure you can imagine how difficult it was for Mom
and Dad to ignore this obnoxious behavior. Most parents
would want to say, "Come on, Mike, you agreed, now
stop acting like a baby!" If Mike continued his misbehavior, they would want to forget the plan and use punishment (which would stop the present obnoxious behavior,
but would not solve the problem of getting the garbage
emptied and allow Mike to learn responsibility).

Mr. and Mrs. Perry continued to ignore Mike's temper tantrum, even when he stomped into the kitchen, got

the garbage, slammed the garage door on his way out, and then sulked and banged his fork on his plate all during dinner.

The next day Mike remembered to empty the garbage and was very pleasant during dinner.

As a result of their consistency in following the agreed-upon plan, Mike did not forget to empty the garbage for two more weeks. When he saw his empty plate turned over again, he said, "Oh, yeah." He then took the garbage out, came to the table, turned his plate over, and pleasantly ate with the rest of the family.

Another reason it is difficult for parents to ignore obnoxious misbehavior is the feeling that they are letting children get away with something. They feel they are actually neglecting their duty to do something about it. This could be true, if there wasn't some plan or purpose behind the ignoring. Mr. and Mrs. Perry let Mike "get away with" his temporary outburst, but since it was part of an agreed-upon plan, they solved the problem of continuous nagging over neglected chores.

Mrs. Beal was frustrated because it irritated her so much when the children would come home from school and dump their books on the couch. Constant nagging was not producing any change.

During a family meeting she told her children she didn't want to yell and nag anymore about this problem. She suggested the nonverbal signal of putting a pillow slip over the television as a reminder that there were books on the couch. The children agreed to this plan, and it worked very well. Mother no longer got involved beyond the signal. When the children saw the pillow slip, they either picked up their own books or reminded someone else to.

Several weeks later, Mrs. Beal wanted to watch her

favorite soap opera after the children had gone to school. She was surprised to find a pillow slip on the television. She looked at the couch and saw the packages she had left there the night before, when she was in a hurry to fix dinner.

The whole family had a good laugh over this turn of events. They enjoyed this technique, and from then on the children thought of many nonverbal signals as solutions to problems.

Mrs. Reed likes to use nonverbal signals in her fifth-grade classroom. She teaches them to her students almost as a second language on the first day of school. One is to have them give her the nonverbal signal of sitting quietly with their hands clasped on top of their desks when they were ready to listen. When she wants them to turn around and sit down during class or an assembly, she raises her right index finger and makes two small circles and then two up and down motions in the air to the rhythm of the words, "Turn around and sit down."

CHOICES

Children often respond to choices when they would not respond to demands. Choices should be respectful and should focus attention on the *needs of the situation.*

Choices are directly related to responsibility. Younger children are less capable of wide responsibility, so their choices are more limited. Older children are capable of broader choices, because they can assume responsibility for the consequences of their choice.

For instance, younger children might be given the choice of going to bed now or in five minutes. Older children might be given full responsibility for choosing their bedtime, because they also take full responsibility for getting themselves up in the morning and off to school without any hassles.

Choices are also directly related to the respect for, and convenience of, others. Younger children might be given the choice of coming to dinner on time or waiting until the next meal to eat, rather than expecting someone to cook and clean up more than once. Older children might be given the choice of being on time or fixing their own dinner and cleaning up any mess they make.

Whenever a choice is given, either alternative should be acceptable to the adult. My first try at choices was to ask my three-year-old, "Do you want to get ready for bed?" She didn't. Obviously, the choice I offered was beyond the need (mine and hers) for her to go to bed, and the choice I offered did not include an alternative I was willing to accept. I waited five minutes and started again by asking, "Would you like to wear your pink pajamas or your blue pajamas?" She chose her blue pajamas and started putting them on.

Children may not have a choice about many things, such as whether or not to do their homework. Homework *needs* to be done, but children can be offered a choice as to when they would like to do it, such as right after school, just before dinner, or after dinner.

"AS SOON AS . . ."

"As soon as you pick up your toys, we will go to the park." This statement is more effective than, "If you pick up your toys, we will go to the park." The first is heard by children as a kind but firm statement indicating what you are willing to do under a prescribed set of circumstances. The latter statement is heard by children (and usually meant by adults) as a challenge to a power contest.

Teachers find it effective to say, "As soon as you are ready, we will begin our lesson."

An attitude of respect for yourself, the child, and the needs of the situation is the key to success in this technique. "As soon as" should be said in a tone of voice that indicates you will withdraw from the situation until the requirements are met. You should then become *unconcerned* and let the child experience the consequences of his or her choice. If you do not become unconcerned, it will become a power contest no matter what words you use.

ALLOWANCE MONEY

Allowances can be a great teaching tool. When children have a regular allowance they can learn the value of money—if parents handle allowances effectively.

Allowance money should not be used for punishment or reward. Many parents use allowance money as leverage to try to make children responsible for their chores. They give out allowances as a reward when chores are done and withhold allowances as a punishment when chores are not done. Children will learn much more about money and responsibility when the threat is taken away. Use family meetings to teach responsibility regarding chores and keep allowances a separate issue.

When children have their own allowance, you can eliminate getting hooked when they see something they want at the store. Whenever Mary says, "I want that!" Her mother replies, "Do you have enough money?" Mary usually doesn't, so Mother says, "Well, maybe you would like to save your allowance so you can buy it."

Mary usually thinks she wants it so bad that she will save her money faithfully until she can buy it. However, it is usually forgotten within hours. She usually doesn't really want it badly enough, even though she would be glad to have Mom spend her money.

As children get older and want an expensive item like a bike, you might have them save ten dollars or more toward the bike. When children have some of their own money invested in things, they are much more responsible about taking care of them.

Children can also use their allowance money to make up for damage they might do to property belonging to someone else.

All of the techniques explained in this chapter can be effective when used and taught in a friendly manner. Your *attitude, intent,* and *manner* are the *keys to success.* Some adults use these techniques in the same manner and for the same purposes as they use punishment. The punitive approach invites rebellion or blind submission. The positive approach invites cooperation, mutual respect, responsibility, and social interest.

QUESTIONS FOR REVIEW OF CHAPTER 9

1. Name and describe several techniques that provide a cooling-off period.

2. What is the rationale for the technique "decide what you will do, not what you will make the children do." Why is it effective?

3. What are the six points to remember to increase the effectiveness of the foregoing techniques?

4. What does it mean to become *unconcerned* when using this technique? What should you do if you cannot become unconcerned?

5. What does it mean to emotionally withdraw?

6. What should always take place after a cooling-off period or any other form of withdrawal?

7. What are the key concepts necessary to avoid morning and bedtime hassles?

8. Why does quality bedtime sharing help avoid bedtime hassles?

9. What are the negative results of getting involved in children's fights?

10. What is the procedure you should follow when you decide to stay out of children's fights?

11. What are the three circumstances when it may not be advisable to stay out of fights?

12. When the decision has been made to get involved in children's fights, what is the most effective technique to use?

13. Explain what it means to "put them in the same boat." What negative results does this help avoid?

14. Explain nonverbal signals. What can be accomplished by using them?

15. Discuss the benefits of giving choices.

16. What are some guidelines for assuring the effectiveness of choices?

17. Discuss the advantages of following the suggestions for allowance money.

18. What are the keys to success in using any of the techniques suggested in this book?

Chapter Ten

LOVE AND JOY IN
FAMILIES AND SCHOOLS

*"Love and joy was just the thing
that he was raised on."*
John Denver

The primary goal of Positive Discipline is to enable both
adults and children to experience more joy, harmony,
cooperation, shared responsibility, mutual respect, and
love in their life and relationships. We often act as
though we have forgotten that love and joy is the whole
point, and find ourselves acting out of fear, judgement,
expectations, blame, disappointment, and anger. Then
we wonder why we feel so miserable.

Following are some reminders that show us how to
avoid detours that keep us from experiencing love and
joy and satisfaction in our relationships.

1. *WHAT* WE DO IS NEVER AS IMPORTANT AS
HOW WE DO IT. The feeling and attitude behind what
we do will determine the "how." The feeling behind
words is often most evident in our tone of voice.

The other day I came home from a trip and was wel-
comed home by a sink full of dirty dishes. I felt dis-

189

couraged and angry and started scolding and criticizing,
"We have agreed that everyone will put their dishes in
the dishwasher. How come no one keeps their agreements when I'm not around."

I looked for someone to blame, but everyone claimed,
"I didn't do it."

From a negative feeling I said, "Okay, we have to have
a family meeting and decide what to do about this."

Can you imagine the outcome if we had tried to have
a family meeting based on my feelings of blame and
criticism? We would not have found the kind of effective
solutions that come from an atmosphere of love and respect. My attacking attitude would have inspired defensiveness and counterattacks instead of harmony.

I realized what I was doing and immediately changed
directions. I could see that my negative attitude would
not produce the results I wanted—to say nothing of how
miserable it made me feel at the time. As soon as I
changed my attitude, my good feelings were accessible
along with inspiration about how to get positive results.

I said to my family, "Let's go out for hamburgers and
enjoy each other. Then we will have a family meeting to
look for solutions instead of blame."

Based on those feelings, we had a very successful family meeting. We laughingly agreed that it must have been
a phantom who had left the dishes in the sink. When we
stopped looking for blame and concentrated on solutions, Mark and Mary came up with a great plan. They
proposed that we would all be assigned two days a week
for KP duty to take care of the phantom's dirty dishes.

Acting from negative thoughts and feelings is a guar-
anteed detour away from love, joy, and positive results.
By dismissing our negative attitudes, we allow our natu-

ral good feelings and common sense, to rise to the sur-
face.

2. SEE MISTAKES AS OPPORTUNITIES TO
LEARN.

In the introduction to this book, I discussed the importance of helping children experience mistakes as opportunities to learn. When adults do not apply this principle
to themselves, it is an immediate detour away from love
and joy and positive results.

Adults could learn the principle of mistakes as opportunities to learn by observing toddlers when they are
learning to walk. Toddlers don't waste time feeling
inadequate everytime they fall. They simply get up and
go again. If they are hurt by the fall, they may cry for a
few minutes before they get on their way again; but they
don't add blame, criticism, or other self-defeating messages to their experience. We can help our children maintain this simple way of experiencing life by rediscovering
the value of mistakes for ourselves.

Thinking we have to be perfect is a well-traveled detour away from love and joy in life. The Three R's of
Recovery can put us back on course.

THE THREE R'S OF RECOVERY

1. Recognize—"Wow! I made a mistake."
2. Reconcile—"I Apologize."
3. Resolve—"Let's work on a solution together."

It is much easier to recognize and take responsibility for
a mistake when it is seen as a learning opportunity rather
than something bad. If we see mistakes as bad we tend

to feel inadequate and discouraged and to become defensive, evasive, judgmental, and critical. On the other hand, when mistakes are seen as opportunities to learn, recognizing them will seem like an exciting venture. "I wonder what I will learn from this one." Self-forgiveness is an important element of the first R of Recovery.

A positive outlook leads naturally to reconciliation. Have you ever noticed how forgiving children are when we are willing to apologize? My children can be feeling angry and resentful about my disrespectful behavior one minute, and switch to total forgiveness as soon as I say I am sorry. "That's okay, Mom. Don't worry about it."

The first two R's of Recovery—recognize and reconcile—create a positive atmosphere which leads naturally to positive solutions. Since I make so many mistakes, the Three R's of Recovery is one of my favorite concepts.

Just recently I said to my eleven-year-old daughter, "Mary, you are a spoiled brat." (The principles of Positive Discipline are always positive, but sometimes I goof.)

Mary said, "Well, don't tell me later that you are sorry."

I said, "You don't have to worry, because I'm not."

I soon realized what I had done and went to her bedroom to apologize. She was still angry and was scribbling "phony" on pages of her copy of *Positive Discipline*. I left the room to give her more time to cool off.

In about five minutes Mary came to me, threw her arms around me and said, "I'm sorry."

I said, "Honey, I'm sorry too. In fact, do you know that when I called you a spoiled brat, I was being one. I was upset at you for losing control of your behavior, but I had lost control of my own behavior. I apologize."

Mary said, "That's okay Mom, I'm sorry for acting like such a brat."

A few days later I overheard Mary on the phone saying to her friend, "Oh Debbie, you are so stupid!" Mary quickly realized what she had done and said, "I'm sorry Debbie. When I call you stupid, that means I am being stupid."

Mary had internalized the principles of Recovery and learned that mistakes are nothing more than wonderful opportunities to learn.

3. SOMETIMES WE HAVE TO LEARN THE SAME THING OVER AND OVER AGAIN.

How many parents have said, "How many times do I have to tell you?"

These parents set themselves up for disappointment and frustration if they don't understand that the answer may be, "Over and over and over." (I often believe that children don't really understand what we try to teach them until they have their own children and try to teach them the same things.)

Mrs. Bordeau expressed such relief in hearing this principle. She said, "I thought that it would take only one family meeting to get my children to cooperate in doing their chores. Since their enthusiasm didn't last longer than a week, I just assumed it wasn't working and went back to daily nagging."

Mrs. Bordeau didn't realize how much progress she had made to get enthusiasm even for a week.

In my family we talk about the issue of chores about every three weeks. The kids will be enthusiastic about their plan for one week; they will follow the plan unenthusiastically for another week; and then do it with lots of complaints for another week. When we discuss chores

again, we will get either renewed committment for the
old plan, or come up with a new plan that creates more
enthusiasm for a while.

I have accepted with gratitude that dealing with chores
once every three weeks is much nicer than daily nagging
and frustration.

Children are not the only ones who need opportunities to learn over and over again. Otherwise, why would
I need to use The Three R's of Recovery so often.

A detour to misery is feeling inadequate or frustrated
everytime we or our children do not learn something
once and for all. The road to love and joy includes not
only acceptance that we will make mistakes but that we
will have opportunities to learn over and over again.

So, Positive Discipline is not about perfection. It is so
gratifying to hear parents say, "My children are still not
perfect, and neither am I, but we sure do enjoy each
other more." These principles do not guarantee perfection—just a whole lot more love and joy along the way.

Adults have the responsibility to help children develop characteristics that will enable them to live happy,
productive lives. It is our job to provide them with a
good foundation that they can build upon. Teaching
them self-discipline, responsibility, cooperation, and
problem-solving skills helps them establish an excellent
foundation. When children exhibit these characteristics
and skills, they will feel a greater sense of belonging and
significance that will manifest itself through positive behavior.

Many techniques have been presented in this book. If
they are seen only as techniques, they will fail. Many
positive attitudes have also been presented. When the
techniques are *put together* with the positive attitudes,

they become concepts that create an atmosphere of love, mutual respect, cooperation, and enjoyment between children.

This chapter includes many concepts that require adult participation and guidance in order to help children develop a strong foundation.

HELPING CHILDREN EXPERIENCE ACCEPTANCE AND APPRECIATION

Every individual yearns to be understood, accepted, and appreciated as a special human being. Helping children experience acceptance and appreciation is one of the most encouraging gifts you can give to help them feel a sense of belonging and significance.

Before you can accept and appreciate children, you must know them well enough to see what there is to accept and appreciate.

GETTING INTO THE CHILD'S WORLD

The first step in getting into a child's world is to remember that *a misbehaving child is a discouraged child.* You cannot really understand another person until you realize that what they *mean* is often quite different from what they say or do. Remember that the misbehaving child *means* to achieve belonging and significance, even though his behavior looks like the opposite.

The Four Steps for Winning Cooperation (which were presented in chapter 6) are excellent for helping you get into the child's world. Use these steps whenever you feel a gap in your communication that is creating hostility and resentment. You will both feel understood after using this process.

Getting into a child's world and helping him feel accepted and appreciated as a person are important cornerstones to the strong foundation we want to help children develop. When they are present, all the other building stones will go more smoothly.

GIVING CHILDREN THE BENEFIT OF THE DOUBT

Every child wants to succeed. Every child wants to have good relationships with others. Every child wants to have a sense of belonging and significance. When we remember this, we will give misbehaving children the benefit of the doubt. Instead of assuming they want to be difficult, we will assume they want positive results and are simply confused about how to achieve them. Our approach will then be based on an attitude of "I know you want to succeed. How can I help?" When we have this attitude, it will be easier to remember the concepts we can use to win cooperation and to help children develop positive characteristics.

TEACHING COMMUNICATION AND PROBLEM-SOLVING SKILLS

When children have good communication and problem-solving skills, they will greatly improve the quality of their interpersonal relationships and life circumstances. The best way to teach these skills is to model them with your own behavior when working with children. *Example is the best teacher.*

Family meetings and class meetings give children and adults the opportunity to practice many communication and problem-solving skills together. If you have been using this process, you have probably noticed your children using skills they learned during the meetings in other areas of their lives.

Some parents and teachers like children to have other options for communication and problem solving when they don't want to wait for a meeting. One possibility is to teach children the following four problem-solving steps when they're trying to resolve a conflict on a one-to-one basis. Children can then choose which one of the steps they would like to use.

1. Ignore it. (It takes more courage to walk away than to stay and fight.)
   a. Do something else. (Find another game or activity.)
   b. Leave long enough for a cooling-off period, then settle it.
2. Talk it over respectfully.
   a. Tell the other person how you feel. Let him know you don't like what is happening.
   b. Listen to what the other person says about how she feels and what she doesn't like.
   c. Share what you think you did to contribute to the problem.
   d. Tell the other person what you are willing to do differently.

3. Agree together on a solution. For example:
   a. Work out a plan for sharing or taking turns.
   b. Apologize.
4. Ask for help if you can't work it out together.
   a. Put it on the agenda.
   b. Talk it over with a parent, teacher, or friend.

After discussing these skills, have the children role-play the following hypothetical situations. Have them solve each of the situations four different ways (one for each of the steps).

· Fighting over whose turn it is to use the tether ball.
· Shoving in line.
· Calling people bad names.
· Fighting over whose turn it is to sit by the window in the car.

Teachers can put these skills on a poster for children to refer to. Some teachers require that children use these steps before they put a problem on the class-meeting agenda.

Mrs. Underwood explained how this works for her. The children in her third-grade class have permission to leave the room at any time to use the problem-solving steps with another person. Quite often she will see two children leave the room and then sees them sitting by the fence talking. A few minutes later they come back to the classroom and go about their business. She has explained to the children that they do not need to share their discussion with anyone else if they don't want to. During class meetings she will ask if anyone would like to share how they have solved a problem. Parents can teach these skills when their children come to them with a problem. Have them wait for a cooling-off period or use the Four Steps for Winning Cooperation so that they will be ready for problem solving. We often talk about these steps during bedtime sharing.

GIVING ENCOURAGEMENT

Encouragement is essential to a good foundation, since children will not grow and progress in positive directions without it. If encouragement were the only concept you learned from this book, it would be significant in improving your relationships with children and in helping them develop a good foundation.

Remember to be encouraging to yourself. Take care of yourself with dignity and respect, or you won't have anything to give.

TEACHING SOCIAL INTEREST

This concept was stressed in the beginning as the key to mental health. Children will find satisfaction and happiness in life if they learn social interest.

All the techniques in *Positive Discipline* are designed to teach children social interest and to allow them to experience social interest from others. This is accomplished most effectively in family and class meetings.

It is impossible to observe an effective class or family meeting without being deeply moved as you witness children engaged in the process of helping each other solve problems in caring and encouraging ways. It is through this process that children develop the long-range characteristics necessary to build a satisfying life.

SEEING THE POSITIVE IN EVERYTHING

Lorrie was suspended from school for having cigarettes in her locker. She told her Dad, "I don't know how they got there! I was just putting them in my pocket to take them to the principal when a teacher came by and sent me to the office." Dad had a hard time believing that Lorrie didn't know how the cigarettes got into her locker, since it has a combination lock. He also found it hard to believe that she was putting them in her pocket to take them to the principal. He felt disappointed that Lorrie would lie to him because they had always been such a close and loving family. He was also worried that she was beginning to ruin her life by getting involved in smoking, drinking, and drugs.

Dad felt like scolding and punishing and letting her know how disappointed he was. Instead he decided to look for the positive. It is never difficult to find, if you are willing to look for it. As he got into Lorrie's world he could understand that she was probably having a tough time deciding how to stick with family values and still be part of the crowd. He also realized that the only reason Lorrie would lie to him would be because she loved him so much she wouldn't want to disappoint him.

With this understanding, Dad approached Lorrie. Instead of scolding and punishing, he kindly said, "Lorrie, I'll bet it is really difficult trying to figure out how to stick up for what you believe and yet not be called a 'party pooper' by your friends."

Lorrie felt such relief as she said, "Yes, it is."

Dad went on, "And, I'll bet that if you would ever lie to us, it would be because you love us so much you wouldn't want to disappoint us." Lorrie got tears in her eyes and could only nod in agreement. Dad added, "Lorrie, we would be disappointed if you did something that would hurt you, but if you don't know that you can always tell us anything, then we aren't doing a good enough job in letting you know how much we love you." Lorrie gave her Dad a big hug, and they just held each other for a while.

They never did directly discuss the problem of smoking and lying. Over a year has gone by, and Lorrie seems to delight in letting her Mom and Dad know everytime she resists the temptation to do something contrary to her values. She also feels proud that she is influencing her friends to stick up for their values.

HELPING CHILDREN DEVELOP A SENSE OF RESPONSIBILITY

The concepts taught in this book help children develop a sense of responsibility. Another point worth repeating is that children will not learn responsibility if adults keep doing for children what they can and should do for themselves.

Parents are not the only ones who do things for children that they could do for themselves. There are many ways teachers could allow children to help. Students would learn more responsibility if teachers would pretend they could not use their arms or legs. Imagine the jobs children would then be allowed to do. They would then feel needed, which would lead to feelings of belonging and significance.

TAKING FULL RESPONSIBILITY YOURSELF

What about adult responsibility? What would happen if adults assumed full responsibility for creating whatever they complain about? I have never seen a power-drunk child without a power-drunk adult close by.

I am not talking about blame. It is not helpful to blame ourselves and feel guilty. It is helpful to be aware of mistakes we might be making so that we can know what to do to correct them and produce the results we want. Whenever we get into power or revenge, do not get into the child's world, do not take time for training, forget to be kind and firm at the same time, use a disrespectful tone of voice, or use any other kind of punishment, we will probably inspire misbehavior in our children.

HAVING COMPASSION FOR YOURSELF

Remember, mistakes are wonderful opportunities to learn! Have compassion for yourself when you make mistakes—and learn from them. I have been learning from mistakes for fifteen years. Even though I make many mistakes, I love these principles because they are wonderful guidelines to help me get back on track everytime I get lost.

Before I learned to have compassion for myself, I was very hard on myself every time I didn't practice what I preach. I would cry on my husband's shoulder, "How can I travel around telling other parents and teachers how to be more effective with children when I don't always do it myself?" He would remind me of other concepts I preach:

- Mistakes are wonderful opportunities to learn.
- Focus on the positive. (I do use these principles at least 80 percent of the time.)
- Have the courage to be imperfect, since it is part of being human.
- Cool off—and then fix it.

Having compassion for yourself means remembering these concepts and continuing to love yourself and love life. With a loving attitude, things will always get better.

PRACTICING RECOVERY SKILLS

The Four Steps for Winning Cooperation can be an excellent part of recovery.

The Dixons went camping in Sequoia National Park with their two children, six-year-old Lucy and nine-year-old Brandon. During a hike, the children were told to stay on the trail. Brandon did not stay on the trail and got lost. When he was found, Mrs. Dixon remained kind and firm as she told Brandon, "We were really worried about you. We love you too much to let you take chances like that. What can we do to make sure it doesn't happen again?" Brandon agreed to stay on the trails, and to give up hiking privileges if he left the trail again.

An hour later Brandon went with a friend to gather wood. They were gone too long, and Mr. and Mrs.

Dixon were worried again. Brandon's friend returned first and reported that Brandon had built a fire out in the forest. Mrs. Dixon blew up. She was not at all respectful as she scolded Brandon and told him she was so disappointed in him that she wasn't sure she could ever trust him again. She then banished him to the camper for the rest of the day.

Mrs. Dixon had been attending a parent study group. She believed in these concepts and felt upset because she had broken all her resolves to follow them. She went for a walk in the forest to cool off. She remembered to have compassion for herself and then decided to use recovery. She asked Brandon to join her in the cab of the camper for a talk. She apologized to Brandon and let him know how bad she felt because she had humiliated him. Brandon said, "That's okay, Mom, I don't blame you." (Children are usually so forgiving when we apologize.)

Mrs. Dixon said, "I really would like to know your side of the story about why you left the trail and why you built the fire."

Brandon explained that he thought he knew the way and added, "Now I know how easy it is to get lost and why it is so important to stay on the trail." He also said that he had seen a television program in which they had built a fire in the forest, and he was doing all the things they had done to be careful. "I buried the fire with a lot of dirt so that it wouldn't start a forest fire."

Mrs. Dixon asked, "Are you aware of some of the things that could have gone wrong before you put the fire out."

Brandon admitted, "Well, I suppose the wind could have blown a spark into some dry leaves."

This gave them the opportunity to talk about the differences between television and real life. Such a nice atmosphere of love and respect had been created between them that Brandon then went on to tell his mother other things which had been bothering him but he had been afraid to talk about. He told her about some of the mischievous things he and some of the kids in the neighborhood were doing. They worked out a plan for Brandon to be a strong leader to help them stay out of trouble. Mrs. Dixon felt that she and Brandon had become much closer because of this experience.

Most people can understand why Mrs. Dixon became angry. They might even think she had every right to scold Brandon and did not owe him an apology. However, anger is understandable and can be expressed respectfully. Humiliation deserves an apology.

The important point is that the mistakes have already been made and cannot be undone. Punishment does not ensure that the misbehavior will not be repeated. It only gives adults a false sense of security that they "have not let them get away with it."

Recovery does not undo the mistakes either, but it does build for the future. Children will hear and learn in an atmosphere of love and respect. Recovery increases trust and closeness, resolves problem situations, and is a model for children that mistakes are opportunities to learn.

CONVEYING UNCONDITIONAL LOVE

Children need to know they are more important than anything they do.

Fred broke one of his mother's prize antique vases.

She was so heartbroken over it that she sat down and cried. Fred felt very bad about what he had done, but finally asked, "Mother, would you feel that bad if something happened to me?"

Children often don't know how important and loved they are. Sometimes parents and teachers focus so much on misbehavior that they lose sight of the child—and the child loses sight of himself.

I was counseling one family whose daughter had stolen some clothing (as a joke, she claimed) from a friend she was mad at. The mother and sister were so upset about this that they were calling her a thief and wondering if there wasn't something basically wrong with her. I asked them why they were so upset. What was their real concern? The mother answered that she was afraid her daughter might end up in Juvenile Hall. I asked why that was a problem. Mother shared that she was concerned about how much that would hurt her daughter.

I then asked the mother how she thought her daughter felt about being called a thief and being accused of having something wrong with her. She admitted that she could see how much she was already hurting her daughter while claiming to be concerned that she would be hurt.

I asked the daughter which she felt would hurt her the most, going to Juvenile Hall or what she was now experiencing with her mother. She said, "This hurts much worse."

Since the daughter is a teenager, there is no way mother can control her. This girl needs to experience the consequences of her behavior, even if it means going to Juvenile Hall. That would be an unpleasant experience, but not nearly as bad as the loss of love and support from her mother.

It is so easy to get things backward so that our intended message is lost. This mother was humiliating her daughter because she loves her and meant to save her from being hurt. All her daughter heard was the humiliation, which she interpreted to mean, "Mother doesn't even like me."

I know you love your children, and you know you love your children, but do they know you love them? You might be surprised if you ask.

One mother asked her three-year-old, "Do you know I really love you?"

The reply was, "Yes, I know you love me if I be good."

A teenager replied to the same question, "I know you love me if I get good grades."

We often nag at our children to do better. We want them to be better because we love them and think they will be happier if they do what we think is good for them.

They usually do not hear that we want them to do better for them. What they hear is, "I can never do anything good enough. I can't live up to your expectations. You want me to be better for you, not for me."

The Four Steps for Winning Cooperation might be helpful when our children doubt the benefits of our suggestions.

1. Getting into the child's world: "Does it seem to you that I want you to get better grades for me or for you?"

2. Show understanding. "I can understand how it might seem like you can't do things good enough for me. When my parents wanted me to do better I felt like I was supposed to live for them and their expectations."

3. Share your real feelings. "I honestly want you to get better grades because I think you would benefit. I know

it can seem like a drag now, but a good education opens many doors to you in the future and offers you more choices."

4. Work on a solution together. "How can we work this out so that you can work on improvement that you see as beneficial to you rather than criticism from me."

Remember that children do better when they feel better. Nothing feels better than unconditional love.

REINFORCING YOUR LEARNING

If you like the concepts presented in *Positive Discipline*, I strongly urge you to read the book again. I guarantee that you will get at least ten times more out of it during a second reading. Repetition is always important for increasing learning, but you will also find that you will see things you totally missed the first time. Many of the puzzle pieces (concepts) presented in the beginning will make more sense because you are now familiar with the rest of the concepts and will be able to put it all together.

I know from personal experience that these concepts really work when they are used correctly. Positive Discipline is an effective and positive way of solving current problem situations. Even more important, it gives children the foundation they need to independently continue building their lives in effective and positive directions.

QUESTIONS FOR REVIEW OF CHAPTER 10

1. What is the primary goal of Positive Discipline?
2. Discuss reasons why "how" we do something is more important than "what" we do. Share personal ex-

amples of how the impact of something you do would be different if you changed "how" you did it.

3. What is the purpose of mistakes?

4. Name and discuss the Three R's of Recovery.

5. How many times can we learn from the same mistake? Discuss whether this applies to all mistakes or if there are some we are justified in feeling bad about.

6. What happens if a technique is used without the proper feelings and attitudes behind it?

7. Why is it so important to "get into a child's world"?

8. What are some effective ways of getting into a child's world?

9. Discuss the four problem-solving steps and how children might benefit from learning them.

10. What is social interest and how do children benefit from learning social interest?

11. What can adults learn from taking full responsibility?

12. What happens if you don't have compassion for yourself? What happens if you do have compassion for yourself?

13. What are the benefits of seeing the positive in everything?

14. Discuss the importance of conveying unconditional love. Discuss the differences between what adults mean and what children hear.

15. Why would anyone want to read a book twice?

Appendixes

PEER COUNSELING

The following article is adapted from the June 1978 issue of *The Guidance Clinic,* Parker Publishing Co., Inc., West Nyack, New York 10994.

This article explains the method used to set up a peer counseling program in two elementary schools, a program organized and supervised by teachers and counselors.

Fifth- and sixth-grade teachers were sent a memo asking them to recommend students who were natural leaders, for participation in a peer counseling training program. The memo read, "We would like to train some peer counselors. Please write down the names of three students you feel are capable leaders, even though their leadership may not now be in a positive direction."

THE TRAINING PERIOD

The recommended students were then interviewed to see if they were interested in making a commitment to go through training and to do peer counseling. It was explained that they would need to volunteer one or two lunch periods per week to do counseling with other students. Those who were interested then completed four training sessions as follows:*

Step One: Making Friends

The entire first training session was devoted to this first step. The students were asked to brainstorm about the most important aspect of friendship and ways to create an atmosphere of trust. They came up with the following:

1. The most important aspect of friendship is an attitude of:
   - Caring
   - Concern
   - Desire to help
   - Respect
2. To create an atmosphere of friendship:
   - Greet the person by name.
   - Tell your name.
   - Show understanding.
   - Tell about yourself. For example, explain your duties as a peer counselor or share an experience

*The steps taught in the training sessions follow the five steps of William Glasser's Reality Therapy. (See William Glasser, M.D., *Reality Therapy: A New Approach to Psychiatry* [New York: Harper and Row, 1975].)

you have had in a situation similar to the referral problem.

· Help the person relax. (Being relaxed yourself helps a lot.)

· Use your sense of humor. (A funny comment or joke is helpful, when appropriate.)

· Express a willingness to work together on solutions that will help solve the problem.

Each student was given a copy of the results of the brainstorming, along with the caution that it was not necessary to use these steps in order or even to use every one of them every time. They were also invited to be creative and add new ideas.

In the second training session the students were taught steps two through five of Reality Therapy.

Step Two: What Are You Doing?

1. Learn specifically what is going on to cause the problem by asking **what, where, when, who,** and **how** questions regarding the problem. These questions usually help the student see his or her part in the problem.

2. Students don't usually start at the beginning, so ask, "What happened before that?" Keep asking this question after each explanation until you feel you have found the beginning.

Step Three: Is It Helping?

Ask the following questions:

1. What are the consequences of what you are doing?
2. What is the payoff? What do you gain?
3. What is the price you pay? What problems does it cause you?

Step Four: Make a Plan to Do Better

What could be done differently to solve the problem?

1. Ask the counselee for suggestions.
2. Offer possible alternatives yourself.

Step Five: Get a Commitment

Ask the counselee:

1. Will you do it?
2. When will you do it?

Role-Playing

The final two training sessions were spent role-playing situations such as:

- A student who has been referred for fighting on the playground.
- A student who has been disrespectful to a teacher.
- A student who refuses to do classwork.

IMPLEMENTATION

At first, peer counseling was done by two students working together with an adult supervisor. As soon as they demonstrated confidence and competency, they worked in pairs as co-counselors without supervision.

Counselees were referred by teachers, who filled out a referral slip with the name of the student and the problem. After seeing the student, the peer counselors were asked to write the solution arrived at on the referral sheet in duplicate. One was returned to the teacher and the other was kept for follow-up and record-keeping purposes.

Most counselees seemed very willing to talk to a peer counselor. The peer counselors showed great insight and skill in zeroing in on the problems and possible solutions, as in the following example.

One of the counselees was having difficulty getting along with a teacher. The peer counselor stated that he understood, because he had once had that problem. The peer counselor then went on to point out that maybe the teacher was having problems and needed some encouragement. He also pointed out that since the student couldn't do anything about the teacher's behavior, he should work on his own. The student and peer counselor worked out a plan for the counselee to be encouraging and to do his work so that the teacher wouldn't have a reason to be upset at him.

Teachers demonstrated enthusiasm and support for the program by referring many students. They also gave credit to the peer counseling program for changing the leadership skills of some of the students from negative to positive.

STARTING A POSITIVE
DISCIPLINE GROUP

"HOW TO" ACHIEVE POSITIVE DISCIPLINE AT HOME AND AT SCHOOL

ATTEND A PARENT STUDY GROUP
LEARN HOW TO HELP CHILDREN DEVELOP:

- Self-discipline
- Responsibility
- Problem-solving skills
- Self-esteem

If you have hassles with children over such problems as:

Fighting
Chores
Homework
Bedtime
Sharing

Responsibility
Mealtime
Getting up and off to
school without nagging

You will learn to understand why children misbehave. You will also learn specific techniques to help solve these problems.

WHEN: Thursday evenings from 7:00 to 9:00 for eight weeks beginning _____

WHERE: School library

. . . .

Cut and return to school

_____ YES, I would like to attend

_____ I am unable to attend on Thursdays, but contact me for another group.

Name _____ Phone _____
Address _____

STUDY GROUP SCHEDULE

Week 1

Introduction: Discuss the principles regarding group explained in the introduction, and in the appendix under "Group Participation."

Birth-order exercise: This exercise, found at the end of chapter 3, is a good get-acquainted activity.

Problem-Solving Form: Pass out several of these to all the group members so that they can remember situations they want to work on in the fourth week.

Reading assignment: The chapters and questions to be discussed next week. (There should be a reading assignment each week corresponding to whatever is on the agenda for the following week.)

Week 2

Chapters 1, 2, and 3.

EXERCISE: Have group members choose a partner and describe a time when they felt one of the Four R's of Punishment. Then invite sharing with large group.

EXERCISE: Take a few minutes to reflect on a situation with a child that might have been different if you had started with a message of love. Share with a partner. Invite sharing with large group.

Discuss the questions at the end of each chapter.

Week 3

Chapters 4 and 5.
Discussion questions.

Week 4

Chapter 6.
Discussion questions.
Problem solving with specific situations. (see pages 225 to 230)

Week 5

Chapters 7 and 8.
Discussion questions.
Problem solving with specific situations.

Week 6

Chapter 9.
Discussion questions.
Problem solving with specific situations.

Week 7

Chapter 10.
Discussion questions.
Problem solving with specific situations.

Week 8

Problem solving with specific situations.

GROUP PARTICIPATION

The value of study groups and some suggestions for group procedure were presented in the introduction. It is further suggested that you might like to present the following ideas at the first meeting.

There are several personalities that may cause problems in groups. They can be avoided when each member is aware of these situations and takes responsibility to cooperate as a group.

THE MONOPOLIZER

I am sure you have had the experience of being in a group with a monopolizer. This can be deadly for everyone else in the group. If you know that this is one of your problems, try the following:

· Count to five before speaking. This gives others a chance for a turn.

· Limit your comments to those you think will be interesting to others, as well as to yourself.

· Make your comments short and to the point. Most monopolizers repeat themselves and summarize several times.

· Make sure you are staying on the subject being discussed.

· Be aware of other group members who may not be as assertive as you are. Help them get into the conversation. (See signs to watch for in the quiet member.)

THE QUIET ONE

After reading about the monopolizer, don't get the idea that you shouldn't talk in a study group. A study group will not be successful without group participation.

There are many reasons why an individual may be a *quiet* member of the group. The two we should be most aware of are: (a) the person who can't get a word in edgewise because of monopolizers; and (b) the person who prefers to remain silent because that is his learning style.

You can tell the difference by watching body language. The person who would like to say something usually leans forward and starts to speak before being drowned out by someone else. She may raise her hand first, whereas others just speak up. More assertive group members can help this person by saying, "Mary, did you have something you wanted to say?"

On the other hand, don't embarrass those who prefer to remain quiet by calling on them when they would prefer not to speak.

THE DEBATOR

Remember that the purpose of a Positive Discipline parent or teacher study group is to learn to understand and practice these concepts. This does not mean it is the only way. However, it is one very effective way to work with children. If time is spent discussing other theories, there will not be time to cover the present theory for full understanding and practical application.

THE SELF-RIGHTEOUS ONE

Some people become so enthusiastic about these principles that they want to convert others immediately. For example, a wife might go home from a study group and say to her husband, "This is the way we are going to do it from now on." A spouse *may* be inspired to try some of these techniques, after having the opportunity to observe the effectiveness of your example, but is *sure* to resist pressure to change.

Of course, it is nice if both adults are working together on the same approach, but it is not necessary. Children are so clever that they can switch their behavior according to the approach of the adult with whom they are interacting. It will not hurt them to experience different approaches from different adults.

The only person you can change is yourself. Use the approach that suits you.

THE DOUBTER ("YES, BUT . . .")

All the techniques suggested in this book have been used successfully by many parents and teachers. Anticipating that something won't work is often a good excuse to avoid trying it out.

While learning, choose only the suggestions you are willing to try. You don't have to buy the whole package to achieve many of the benefits.

PROBLEM-SOLVING FORM

Describe the problem interaction in detail. (When was the last time it happened?)

How did it make you feel? (Irritated, threatened, hurt, or inadequate.)

What did you do in response to the child's behavior?

What was the child's response to what you did?

What is your guess about the child's mistaken goal?

What are some alternative suggestions you could try the next time the problem occurs? (Record suggestions from the group here.)

USING THE PROBLEM-SOLVING FORM

It is a good idea to make several copies of the Problem-Solving Form for each member of the group. During the first few weeks of the group, this will help group members remember the situations they would like to discuss after learning the basic concepts in the first six chapters of this book.

When it is time to discuss these situations, have the group guess the mistaken goal. Group members should attempt to get at the primary feelings of the adult. Listen for tone of voice and discrepancies. Does the adult claim slight annoyance or inadequacy when his tone of voice and description of the problem indicate power—a desire to make the child do it his way? Is anger or frustration a cover-up for feeling threatened or hurt?

Once the mistaken goal has been determined, the group should give several suggestions for the parent or teacher to try. These suggestions should include as many concepts and techniques as possible, including some specific ideas for encouragement. The person with the problem can then choose one or more of these ideas to try.

The next group meeting should begin with a report on the effectiveness of the suggestions. If the suggestions were not effective, the group will usually be able to help the person understand why. For example, he may have forgotten to use a respectful tone of voice or he may not have waited for a cooling-off period.

Following are some examples of situations that were presented to a group and the solutions that were suggested.

Six-year-old Matt always thinks things are unfair. One morning while Mom was talking to Matt, she reached down to smooth out the bedspread on his younger brother's bed. Matt said, "That's not fair. You always help him and not me." Mom shared with the group that she felt annoyed. Further questioning from the group revealed that she felt hurt. She tries so hard to be fair, but Matt accuses her of being unfair. The group then guessed that Matt was also feeling hurt because of his perception that Mom favored his younger brother. They came up with two suggestions:

1. Use the Four Steps for Winning Cooperation. Verbalize what you think he is feeling. Share a time you yourself felt things were unfair. Let him know you understand. Explain your desire to be fair because of equal love for both. Seek a solution, with Matt's help, as to what can be done.

2. Spend special time with Matt. This could be part of the solution.

Mrs. James shared her concern because her first-grade student, Scott, had developed a pattern of not completing his work. She initially thought his goal must be either attention or power, because she knew he is very capable, as shown by past performance. One suggestion from the group was to do goal disclosure with Scott, which would at least give Mrs. James more feedback as to what his goal was. Mrs. James wanted some practice with this technique, so she role-played Scott while another member of the group did goal disclosure. As she got into Scott's world, she was amazed to discover that his goal was probably revenge. She was also a close friend of Scott's family and realized the problem had started after she had taken some time off for a vacation. Scott had shared real concern with his parents that she might not come back. Since this really hurt him, he was afraid to get too close when she did come back. Instead, his behavior indicated passive revenge. Mrs. James was eager to try goal disclosure with Scott so that they could then talk about this and do some problem solving—after the steps of winning cooperation.

Mrs. Roberts, a preschool teacher, shared her problem with Steven, who always played in the block area but wouldn't help pick them up. At first Mrs. Roberts felt she was just frustrated but came to realize it was because she couldn't make him do what he should do. After identifying the goal as power, the group came up with the following suggestions:

1. Take time for training. Make sure he knows exactly what is expected.

2. Ask questions: "Do you like to play in the blocks? What are you supposed to do when finished? How many blocks do you think you can pick up during clean-up time?"

3. Give a choice, including a logical consequence. Would you like to pick up the blocks now or during story time? Would you like to pick up the blocks or give up the privilege of playing with the blocks?

4. Redirect power behavior. Let him be in charge of clean-up.

Mrs. Roberts chose the fourth alternative as the one she thought would appeal to Steven and solve the problem.

Mrs. Sedgewick complained about six-year-old Scott not respecting his toys and picking them up. It was clear to the group that her voice indicated power that was escalating to revenge. The following possibilities were suggested by the group:

1. "Own" the problem. Share how much it bothers you to see the toys cluttering the house. Admit that you may have purchased more toys than he wants or needs.

2. Ask for help and solutions to your problem.

3. Take time for training and organization. Make drawstring bags or get ice-cream cartons for different sets of toys. Get agreement from Scott that only one bag or carton can be down at a time, that one must be picked up before another one is used.

4. Give a choice. Either he can pick them up or you will. If you pick them up, they stay up until he shows enough interest and responsibility. If this doesn't happen, then he definitely has too many toys to care.

PROBLEM-SOLVING POSSIBILITIES

The following is a list of some concepts that will be effective with most behavior problems. Whenever a group member asks for help with a specific situation, see how many of them would be appropriate suggestions.

1. Having a cooling-off period

2. Going through the Four Steps for Winning Cooperation

3. Redirecting the misbehavior into contributing behavior

4. Ignoring the problem and scheduling special time

5. Taking time for training

6. Putting the problem on the agenda

7. Getting the child involved in a solution, including an agreement and a logical consequence

8. Seeing the positive and responding accordingly

9. Focusing on the 80 percent that is positive and expressing appreciation

10. Making sure that the message of love gets through

11. Taking full responsibility

12. Practicing recovery

Be sure to have the person who presented a problem write down all suggestions and circle the one (or more) he or she wants to try.

Class Meeting
Observation Form:

To be used for helpful feedback only—for self or peer observation.

Instructions: Make a check to tally every time the specified behavior is observed.

Behavior   Number of Times Observed

Statements (Effective):
    Courtesy (Please, thank you, you're welcome, etc.)   _____

Statements (Ineffective):
    Censoring (We have already solved a problem like that, etc.)   _____
    Judgmental (I agree, I don't agree, etc.)
    Lecturing or moralizing (It is disrespectful to interrupt. You'll never learn if you cheat, etc.)   _____

Questioning Skills (Very effective):
    Finding the positive (Did it help you out? How many think it is great that people want to pass? etc.)   _____
    Asking opinions (How many think it is okay to cheat? Not okay? etc.)   _____
    Redirecting negatives (What does it feel like to be a new kid in school? Which of these suggestions are helpful and which hurtful? etc.)   _____

Sense of Humor (Very effective)   _____

Teacher _____   Evaluator _____
Grade _____ School _____ Date _____

A LITTLE IMPERFECTION

by Kathy Schinski

A little imperfection is not so bad.
A little imperfection shouldn't make you feel sad.
It keeps you in touch with reality
And with all the not so perfect people
Just like me.

A little imperfection is not so tough.
You need a little of it to be perfect enough.
It puts your feet back on the earth
And lets the other people keep
Their own self-worth.

A little imperfection in just the perfect place
Can make this not so perfect world easier to face,
More of us could go in the right direction
If we could learn to put up with a little imperfection.

A little imperfection is not so bad.
A little imperfection shouldn't make you feel sad.
It keeps you in touch with reality
And with all the not so perfect people
Just like me.

SUGGESTED READINGS

Many groups find they would like to continue meeting for mutual support, encouragement, and education. You might like to continue to study some of the other books I've listed. They are all excellent and will help you increase your knowledge and skills.

Adler, Alfred. *What Life Should Mean to You.* New York: G. P. Putnam's Sons, 1958.

Allred, G. Hugh. *How to Strengthen Your Marriage and Family.* Provo, Utah: Brigham Young University Press, 1976.

————. *Mission for Mother: Guiding the Child.* Salt Lake City, Utah: Book Crafts, 1968.

Corsini, R. J., and G. Painter. *The Practical Parent.* New York: Harper & Row, 1975.

Dinkmeyer, D., and Rudolph Dreikurs. *Encouraging*

233

Children to Learn: The Encouragement Process. Englewood Cliffs, N.J.: Prentice-Hall, 1963.

Dinkmeyer, D. and G. McKay. *Raising a Responsible Child.* New York: Simon & Schuster, 1973.

Dreikurs, Rudolph. *Social Equality: The Challenge of Today.* Chicago: Contemporary Books, Inc., 1971.

Dreikurs, Rudolph, R. Corsini, and S. Gould. *Family Council.* Chicago: Henry Regnery, 1974.

Dreikurs, Rudolph, and L. Grey. *A New Approach to Discipline: Logical Consequences.* New York: Hawthorn Books, Inc., 1968.

Dreikurs, Rudolph, B. Grunwald, and F. Pepper. *Maintaining Sanity in the Classroom.* New York: Harper & Row, Inc., 1971.

Dreikurs, Rudolph, and V. Soltz. *Children: The Challenge.* New York: Hawthorn Books, Inc., 1964.

Forer, Lucille. *The Birth Order Factor.* New York: McKay, 1976.

Glenn, H. Stephen, J. Nelsen. *Raising Self-Reliant Children in a Self-Indulgent World.* Rocklin CA: Prima Publishing, 1987.

Kvols-Riedler, K. and B. *Redirecting Children's Misbehavior.* Boulder, Colo.: R.D.I.C. Publications, 1979.

Lund, J. L. *Avoiding Emotional Divorce.* Orem, Utah: Noble Publishing, Inc., 1982.

Nelsen, Jane. Understanding: *Eliminating Stress and Dissatisfaction in Life and Relationships.* Fair Oaks, CA: Sunrise Press, 1986.

Walton, F. X. *Winning Teenagers Over.* Adlerian Child Care Books, P.O. Box 210206, Columbia, S.C. 29221.

Index

Adler, Alfred, 21
Adlerian psychology
  basic concepts, 23–29
    belongingness/
      significance, 24
    children as social
      beings, 23
    equality, 27
    goal orientation of
      behavior, 23–24
    love, 28–29
    misbehavior as
      discouragement,
      24–25
    social interest, 25–27
  birth-order, 31–45
Adlerian study group
  announcement for, 219
  debator in, 223–24
  doubter in, 224
  monopolizer in, 222–23
  problem-solving form,
    225–29
  problem solving options,
    229–30
  quiet one in, 223
  schedule for, 220–22
  self-righteous one in, 224
Adult-child interactions,
  11–12
  kindness/firmness,
    importance of, 78–79
  misguided adults, example
    of, 76–78

  mutual sharing, setting
    time for, 100–102
  permissiveness, 11, 13
  positive discipline, 11
  strictness, 11, 13
Agenda
  class meetings, 121–22,
    124, 130, 134, 136
  family meetings, 150
Allowance money, 186–87
"As soon as . . ." statement,
  185–86
Assumed inadequacy,
  remedy for, 51, 54
Attention, remedy for, 50,
  52
Avoiding Emotional Divorce
  (Lund), 105

Bathroom technique,
  cooling-off period,
  160–61
Bedtime hassles, 172–75
  bedtime mutual sharing,
    102, 174–75
Behavior
  goal orientation of, 23–24
  mistaken goals of, 46–62
    assumed inadequacy,
      46, 47, 49
    attention, 46, 47, 49
    and degree of
      discouragement,
      57–61

goal disclosure, 55–57
identifying mistaken
goals, 48, 55–57
mistaken goal chart, 64
power, 46, 47, 49
remedies for, 50–55
revenge, 46, 47, 49
and teenagers, 61–62
primary goal of, 47
Birth-order, 31–45
and children's fights,
177–78
and educational
evaluation, 40–42
family environment and,
39
gender and, 37–38
group exercise, 44–45
and marriage, 42–43
middle children, 36, 42,
44
oldest children, 33–34,
37, 42, 43
only children, 36
perception/interpretation
of child, 32–33
and role of child, 32
role swapping and, 38–39
and teaching style, 43–44
time span between
children and, 38
usefulness of concept, 33,
37, 40–42
youngest children, 34–36,
42, 44

Chairpersons
class meetings, 140
family meetings, 148

Children
Adlerian concepts related to
belongingness/
significance, need for,
24
and equality, 27
goal orientation of
behavior, 23–24
love, need for, 28–29
misbehavior as
discouragement,
24–25
as social beings, 23
and social interest,
26–27
as good perceivers/poor
interpreters, 23–24,
32
modern child, 8–10
societal changes and,
9–10
success, perceptions/skills
needed for, 10–11
winning over children,
effects of, 22
Choices, 184–85
and needs of situation,
184–85
Chores, family meetings,
155–56
Class meetings, 114–43
agenda
use of, 121–22, 124,
130, 134, 136
use as revenge, 136
attributes/actions to
avoid, 115–16
chairpersons, 140
circle, sitting in, 122–23

and classroom planning
    decisions, 140–41
cooling-off period and,
    122
decision making, 116,
    124, 125
effectiveness of, 115
ending meeting, 142
frequency of, 116, 137
ganging-up problem,
    132–33
goals of, 117–20
    compliments, 118–19,
        123
    logical consequences,
        teaching of, 119–20,
        124–25, 130–32,
        142
    mutual respect, teaching
        of, 117–18
observation form, 231
parent objections, 138
questions/answers related
    to, 130–39
secret pal option, 140
structure of, 123–26
teacher's role, 126–30
    modeling courtesy, 126
    nonjudgmental attitude,
        129
    open-ended
        questioning,
        developing, 126–27
    ownership of problems,
        128–29, 134–35
    positive intent, finding,
        129–30
with younger children,
    139

Communication/problem
    solving skills
    teaching of, 196–99
        problem solving steps,
            197–98
        role-playing, 198
Compliments
    family meetings, 149
    praise vs. encouragement,
        103–5, 110–11
    use during class meeting,
        118–19, 123
Cooling-off period, 65, 88,
    160–66
    bathroom technique,
        160–61
    child's refusal during,
        166
    emotional withdrawal,
        170–71
    isolation technique,
        75–76, 163–66
    novel technique, 161–63
    temper tantrums, 19
Criticism
    constructive criticism, 105
    vs, encouragement,
        105–6, 110–11

Decision making, class
    meetings, 116, 124,
    125
Discouragement, and
    misbehavior, 63,
    87
Disruptive behavior, and
    leadership skills, 97
Dreikurs, Rudolph, 21, 23,
    35, 46, 72, 78, 88

Educational evaluation, and
        birth order, 40–42
Emotional withdrawal,
        170–71
Encouragement, 87–112,
        199
    childhood memories, use
        of, 111–12
    Four Steps to Winning
        Cooperation, 89–92
    case examples, 90–92
    group exercises, 110–12
    improvement vs.
        perfection, 95–97
    and mutual respect,
        92–94
    mutual sharing, special
        time for, 100–102
    redirecting misbehavior,
        97–100
    and timing, 88–89
    vs. criticism, 105–6,
        110–11
    vs. praise, 103–5, 110–11

Family environment, and
        birth order, 39
Family meetings, 144–59
    agenda, 150
    chairperson, 148
    chores, 155–56
    compliments, 149
    format for, 147–48
    gratitude, sharing of,
        149
    messy house example,
        144–47
    planning activities,
        150–55
    problem solving, 150

    secretary, 148
    single parents, 158–59
    teenagers, 157–58
    younger children, 156–57
Fights (children's), 177–81
    and birth order, 177–78
    when to intervene, 179
Firmness, importance of,
        78–79
Four Steps to Winning
        Cooperation, 89–92
    case examples, 90–92

Ganging-up problem, class
        meetings, 132–33
Gender, and birth order,
        37–38
Glenn, Dr. Stephen, 10
Gratitude, sharing of, family
        meetings, 149

Humiliation, of children by
        adults, 13, 22, 27

Imperfection, positive use
        of, 110
Improvement, vs.
        perfection, 95–97
Isolation technique,
        cooling-off period,
        163–66

Kindness, importance of,
        78–79

Logical consequences
    children's responses to,
        79–80
    class meetings, 119–20,
        124–25, 130–32, 142

difficulties in use of, 78,
    83–84
isolating child, 75–76
kindness/firmness and,
    78–79
teacher's use of, 81
times to avoid use of, 84
Love
    conveyed to children,
        28–29
    unconditional love, 205–8
Lund, Dr. John, 105

Marriage, and birth order,
    42–43
Mealtime hassles, 175–77
Middle children, 36, 42,
    44
Misbehavior
    adult responses to, 48,
        55–57, 63, 64
    and discouragement, 63,
        87, 195
    goals of
        assumed inadequacy,
            46, 47, 49
        attention, 46, 47, 49
        identifying goals, 48,
            55–57
        power, 46, 47, 49
        revenge, 46, 47, 49
    recovery, 191–95
    redirecting misbehavior,
        95–96
    focus on positive,
        95–97, 108
    Four Steps to Winning
        Cooperation, 89–92
    group exercises,
        110–12

imperfection, positive
    use of, 110
making up for it, 98
question approach, 109
self-evaluation by child,
    108
and social pressure,
    98–100
training/teaching of
    children, 106–8
remedies for, 50–55
worsening of, 18, 81,
    142

Natural and logical
    consequences, 68–85
logical consequence,
    meaning of, 69
logical consequences
    case example, 72
    children's responses to,
        78–80
    difficulties in use of, 78,
        83–84
    isolating child, 75–76
    kindness/firmness and,
        78–79
    reasonableness in, 73
    related consequence,
        73
    respect in, 73
    teacher's use of, 81
    times to avoid use of,
        84
long-term effects of, 85
natural consequences
    case examples, 69–70
    meaning of, 68–69
    times to avoid use of,
        71–72, 84

Nonverbal signals, 181–84
  ignoring misbehavior,
    181–84
Novel technique, cooling-off
    period, 161–63

Oldest children, 33–34, 37,
    42, 44
Only children, 36

Pampering
  effects of, 35–36
  reasons for, 35
Peer counseling, 213–17
  implementation, 217
  training period, 214–16
Perfection
  imperfection, positive use
    of, 110
  vs. improvement, 95–97
Permissiveness, 11, 13, 78
  case example, 16–17
Positive, focus on positive,
    95–97, 108, 200–201
Positive discipline, 11
  allowance money, 186–87
  "as soon as . . ."
    statement, 185–86
  for bedtime hassles,
    172–75
  benefit of doubt, giving to
    child, 196
  case example, 18–19
  for children's fights,
    177–81
  choices, 184–85
  class meetings, 114–43
  communication/problem
    solving skills,

  teaching of, 196–99
  and compassion for self,
    202–3
  cooling-off period, 160
  emotional withdrawal,
    170–71
  encouragement, 87–112
  family meetings, 144–59
  guidelines for success,
    168–70
  long-range effects, 19
  love, unconditional love,
    205–8
  for mealtime hassles,
    175–77
  for morning-time hassles,
    171–72
  natural and logical
    consequences, 68–85
  nonverbal signals, 181–84
  recovery skills, 203–5
  reinforcement of learning,
    208
  responsibility, developing
    in children, 201–2
  rule making, child's
    participation, 19
  side-effect, misbehavior
    gets worse, 18, 81,
    142
  social interest, teaching
    of, 199–200
  vs. traditional methods,
    13–19
  See also Redirecting
    misbehavior; specific
    topics.
Power struggle, remedy for,
    51, 52–53

Praise
  characteristics of, 103–4
  comments, evaluation of,
    105
  negative effects of, 103
  vs. encouragement,
    103–5, 110–11
Problem-solving
  family meetings, 150
  skills, teaching of, 196–99
Punishment
  long-term effects of,
    13–14, 74
    resentment, 74, 77
    retreat, 74
    revenge, 74, 77
  misconceptions about, 67
  power of parent and, 74,
    76
  and revenge, 67–68
  suffering of child as goal,
    75, 76, 78
  vs. natural and logical
    consequences, 68–69

Raising Children for Success
  (Glenn), 10
Recovery, 191–95
  practicing recovery skills,
    203–5
  recognition in, 191–92
  reconciliation in, 192
  resolution, 193–94
Redirecting misbehavior
  focus on positive, 95–97,
    108
  Four Steps to Winning
    Cooperation, 89–92
  group exercises, 110–12

imperfection, 110
  making up for it, 98
  question approach, 109
  self-evaluation by child,
    108
  and social pressure, 98–100
  training/teaching of
    children, 106–8
Resentment, and
  punishment, 74, 77
Respect (mutual), 92–94
  attitudes in, 92
  case example, 92–94
  teaching of, class
    meetings, 117–18
Responsibility, developing
  in children, 201–2
Retreat, and punishment, 74
Revenge
  and punishment, 74, 77
  remedy for, 51, 53
Role in family, and birth
  order, 37–38

Secret pal option, class
  meetings, 140
Sharing (mutual)
  and bedtime routine, 102
  bedtime sharing, 174–75
  case example, 101
  effects of, 101–2
  setting time for, 100–102
Single parents, family
  meetings, 158–59
Social interest
  example of, 25–26
  and fourteen-day cure
    plan, 26
  teaching of, 199–200

Social pressure, redirecting
   misbehavior and,
   98–100
Society, modern, changes
   effecting children,
   8–10
Strictness, 11, 13
   case example, 15–16
   punishment, long-range
     results of, 13–14
Success, perceptions/skills
   needed for, 10–11

Teacher's role
  class meetings
    modeling courtesy, 126
    nonjudgmental attitude,
     129
    open-ended
     questioning, 126–27

  ownership of problems,
   128–29, 134–35
  positive intent, 129–30
Teenagers
  family meetings, 157–58
  mistaken goals of
   behavior, 61–62
Temper tantrums,
  cooling-off, 19
Timing, and use of
  encouragement,
  88–89

Unconditional love, 205–8

Younger children
  class meetings, 139
  family meetings, 156–57
Youngest children, 34–36,
  42, 44

Study Group Aids are available from Sunrise
Press. For more information, please call or write to:
Sunrise Press
P.O. Box 788
Fair Oaks, CA 95628
1-800-456-7770